About the Au

You might wonder why you'd be interested in my life; I'm no celebrity, although I have a famous name. I've had a scandalous childhood but carry on with my head held high regardless. In later life I put my heart into ethnic minority charity work and as a result found myself in Buckingham Palace shaking Queen Elizabeth's hand and accepting an MBE, one of the proudest moments of my life. I saw this book as my personal healing. I'm sharing my childhood with you in the hope that it will inspire abuse victims to never give up striving for personal happiness; what doesn't kill you will eventually make you stronger.

Dedication

This book is dedicated to my dear sister Nancy and brother Michael, who have passed away and left a big hole in my heart. Never forgotten.

Bridget Jones MBE

FINDING MY FREEDOM

AUTOBIOGRAPHY

AUSTIN MACAULEY PUBLISHERS™
LONDON • CAMBRIDGE • NEW YORK • SHARJAH

Author Note: I have tried to recreate events, locales and conversations from my memories of them. In order to maintain their anonymity in some instances I have changed the names of individuals and places, I may have changed some identifying characteristics and details such as physical properties, occupations and places of residence.

A CIP catalogue record for this title is available from the British Library.

ISBN 9781528987707 (Paperback)
ISBN 9781528917865 (Hardback)
ISBN 9781528987714 (ePub e-book)

www.austinmacauley.com

First Published (2020)
Austin Macauley Publishers Ltd
25 Canada Square
Canary Wharf
London
E14 5LQ

Acknowledgements

I would like to thank my daughter Kellyanne Jones for helping me to write and complete this autobiography.

Author's Note

I know some folks may find this book a hard read, but this was my childhood from the ages of three and a half to sixteen years.

I have changed some names and places to protect the rest of the family, This is my story, this is how I see it and this is how I wrote it. I'm an uneducated gypsy woman; if you read mistakes or things don't make sense, neither did my life.

* * *

I didn't write for sympathy. I'm not a victim, I am a survivor and hope my book helps those who may have suffered like me.

Don't let your past stop you from achieving your dreams. Hold your head up high, let go of whatever holds you back: that's the only way you'll ever find your freedom.

Table of Contents

Prologue

As I stood over him, tears running down my face, anger burning within my stomach, I wondered: *Why hadn't I the guts to confront him when he was alive? Why was I at his funeral?* Maybe I was making sure he was dead.

My head was screaming, *Rot in Hell, you fucking bastard.*

I hadn't seen my mother for years, who was now kneeling down beside my father's open grave, sobbing so bad as if her heart was breaking.

Not surprisingly, I was the only daughter who had attended my father's burial.

I had lived in Manchester for some years, but never had the courage to return to the ugly house. With Father out of the way now, I felt strong enough.

The Victorian terraced house looked so innocent as it looked back at me. I couldn't believe it was still standing. All the pain and abuse that I and my siblings had suffered in this house came flooding back. How long I stood there staring at it I can't remember, but it must have been quite some time.

The front door opened. A small, dumpy woman asked if she could help us.

"No, thank you," I replied. "It's just that I knew the family that once lived here."

"Crazy load of feckers, if you ask me. The kids set the house alight. Crazy," said the woman.

Crazy maybe, but that action saved our lives, I thought.

Police

It was a cold autumn night in Moate, Southern Ireland. A soft rain was falling. All was quiet on my gypsy camp, except the sound of raindrops falling on the leaves of the big ash trees and the occasional bark of one of the family's pet dogs.

I stirred in my sleep and was aware of my mother's warm body sleeping beside me.

Suddenly, both of us were awake. Lights, lots of them, flashing in the windows of our wagon.

"Who the feck is that?" Mother called out. Someone was banging impatiently on our door.

Angry voices were screaming, "Open up the fecking door! Come on!" The angry voices kept yelling.

"Get your fecking dirty gypsy arses off this land," another said. "We don't need your kind of scum around here."

A woman put her ugly face to our window and told my mother to move now, or else she was going to burn us all alive in the wagon.

I stood in our wagon, terrified with fear and holding very tightly to my mother's arm. "Please, I beg ye, in the name of Jesus Christ, go away and leave us alone until the sun rises, then we gladly be on our way," Mother said.

The woman didn't take any notice of my mother's pleading. Instead, she began kicking down our wagon door, so my mother had no choice but to let her in.

Mother called her a fecking old bastard and said, "Why can't ye cunts leave us alone? What harm are we doing? We are just camping here. It's only a piece of land, for God's sake."

The woman grabbed her by her arm, pulling her outside and pushed her onto the wet ground as if Mother was some wild animal. The rest of the police laughed at her.

I ran to my mother's rescue to help her up from the ground. As I did this, I kicked out at the person who had hurt my mother and ended up flat on my arse. Mother was still on the soggy, muddy ground. I managed to get myself up but was covered in mud.

I was wishing I had grabbed Mother's big black coat for her as I ran out of the wagon to save her. It was freezing cold and had been raining all night. I knew how she disliked the cold weather. The rest of the families who were camping with us knew better than to interfere, because they would have all been arrested.

It took the families around a few hours before they were ready to move. There were no authorised gypsy sites in Ireland at that time. Our family would spend hours on end looking for somewhere suitable to pull to. The council did find a place for us, but it was only for a few weeks. This would give the men from our camp time to seek out some work to provide for their families.

My drunken father would leave the new camp with his horse and cart and be absent for days on end. My aunt Catalan said he didn't have the mentality to realise that he had responsibilities to his young wife and his half a dozen children to provide for. It wasn't uncommon for him to come home drunk without a penny in his pocket and get rowing with Mother because there was no food left over for him, once she had fed the children and herself with what little food she had, and he had the cheek to beat her over this.

He was a very cruel, nasty person and why Mother put up with him, only God knows.

If it wasn't for Mother's sister, Mary Helen, who would go out begging and telling fortunes to help my mother out, us kids wouldn't have survived.

My aunt was my mother's older sister. She was a lovely woman with a heart of gold. All the food she got from begging from houses she would cook on the open fire outside our tents for her nieces and nephews. She couldn't read or write like some of her family, but what a clever woman she was! She could put her hand to anything and it would turn out good. As for telling fortunes, she was the best. She only had to put her finger on your forehead and she could tell you everything about you and your future.

She had beautiful, long, raven-black hair, and bright blue eyes that looked into your soul. She was thirty-two years old, and still not married. It was quite unusual for a woman at that age not to be married in our travelling community. There were rumours that she was barren, plus no man wanted to marry her because she couldn't be controlled by them.

When drunken Father used to beat up on my mother, Aunty Mary Helen would attack him. She would tell him he had no right to beat up on any woman, let alone her sister; but as far as he was concerned, she was his wife and he could do what he liked with her. Many times he'd be walking around with black eyes or scratches on his face. When asked by other travellers who didn't live in our camp who the feck had he been fighting with again, he made up stories saying he had a fight with a few Gorgie (non Travellers) he knew. He'd be the laugh of the town if he said it was his sister-in-law.

Aunt Mary Helen was my favourite of all my other aunties, not just because she was always shoving food down my throat to make me big and strong, but she was like a second mother to our family. Some nights I was allowed to sleep in her tent overnight, especially if she was taking me out early in the morning with her begging. Her routine was always the same: up at the crack of dawn, clean her tent up, and get everyone else up. Not that they asked her to call them up, it was just something she did. She was up, everyone else had to be.

"Come on, little person." That was her nickname for me, because I was quite small in height for my three and a half years, compared to the rest of my siblings when they were my age. "The Devil will not wait for no man, places to go, money to be earned," she'd be muttering under her breath as she walked down the street like a sergeant major and me barely able to keep up with her.

"Jesus, Mary and Joseph! I swear the little leprechauns can walk faster than you. No matter," she'd say, "I want you to look, listen and learn, my girl, from me, so when you grow up, you can make a living for yourself and won't have to depend on any man. Are you taking heed of me, my girl?"

I didn't understand a word she was on about, but politely said, "Yes."

My family were Irish Tinkers, also known as travellers. Some people called us gypsies, tramps, edge bumpers and pikeys. My family were hounded from place to place because of who we were. I knew from a very early age that the police and village people hated us because my aunt Rose told me so. She said they were frightened of people like us, because we were different from them; and, if the truth be told, the country folk were jealous of us and believed our lives were romantic, with our wagons and colourful horses, plus the freedom to move wherever we liked.

"Them gorger lot should try living with us for a few days. They'd soon see they have feck all to envy of us for," Aunt Rose would say.

"Freedom! My big fat arse!" cried my auntie June. "We were attacked day and night by them bastards –" she meant the police – "and the fecking villagers lot, they would come to our camps and burn down our fecking tents to the ground. Our men can't fight them cunts back. If they did, they'd be arrested, locked up for days without even being charged, because them bastards knew there was nothing they could charge the men for. Our children were not allowed to go to school because the gorgers would threaten to take their children out of schools if any gypsy kids were accepted in them. Their solution to sort out the problem with the pikey kids was to put us all up against the wall and shoot the lot of us like wild animals."

My mother was forever telling my aunts not to talk around me because I had big ears and had a bad habit of repeating what I'd heard. Best to keep their tongues behind their teeth when *she's* around, meaning me.

"Only the other day, Father Doyle came to my tent about Kelly's first Holy Communion. Bridie told him that her drunken daddy was taken away by the bastards for not paying his fee for pissing up someone's wall. The poor man went red in the face. He coughed so much I thought he was going to have a heart attack," my mother said.

I remember standing there looking at Mother and wondering why she was angry with me.

"What did the priest say to her?" Aunt June asked my mother.

"Well, he asked her who the bastards were. Bridie told him they are the Gorgie people who are nasty and all dressed the same in black uniforms and have the same names. He was doing his best to explain that the people she was referring to are called the Garda, policemen, not bastards, but she was having none of it because Aunt Mary Helen said they are all bastards. It must be true because she said so, and her aunt knows everything," my mother said.

"That's my girl," laughed Auntie Mary Helen. "Better the children need to know the police's hate for us. Look, they come to our camps. The devastation and misery they cause is unbelievable. They expect our family to treat them with respect just because who they are but show no respect for us gypsies."

I may have only been three and a half years old, but I do remember the hatred the police had towards gypsies. They would come to our camps before daybreak and expect us to move there and then, whatever the weather, be it raining or snowing. My poor brothers and sisters would be dragged from their tents, still half-asleep, and be expected to round up the chickens, dogs, and what other animals they could catch in the dark. My parents would always be in a mad rush to get the horses harnessed and hitched up to the wagons, ready for the move. My parents rode with the youngest children on the wagons, while the older ones would have to walk behind, carrying the bedclothes and, of course, the grumpy animals, who didn't take too kindly to being disturbed.

I always asked my aunt Mary Helen where were we going to live and whether people would hate us there.

"I don't know, baby girl. Don't know why you ask me that question when we are shifted on. My answer to you will be the same: fuck knows," said Auntie.

I didn't understand why all the camps were called the same names, but I hoped that it would be a lot better than the one we were leaving behind us. Still, every new one would be the same: extremely muddy. Us children could not play out because some of them were rat-infested, and we'd be stuck in the tents and wagons for days on end until the men of the camps found a better place to move on to. Our poor horses weren't that keen to be standing on muddy fields as well. Our men folk would spend hours struggling to get them and the wagons on the fields, but in the end, the horses would realise their owners were masters, not the other way around.

I didn't mind being moved on because I could help my sisters put the tents up. Not that they needed it. I was more of a hinder than a helper, and anyway, they had no choice. If they didn't let me help, I would go running to my aunt Mary Helen and tell her my sisters were being horrible to me, which of course, wasn't true. People said Mary Helen had a tongue like a sword and could cut you to pieces in seconds with it, so more or less, I got my own way within our camps.

My parents may not have shown me any love or affection, but Mary Helen made up for it in many ways.

Our tents (known as benders) were made up of willow wood. The sticks of wood would be kept in water to make them very flexible to bend and shape. Once the wood was up, it would be covered with waterproof woven material. If the weather was very cold, a fire would be built inside the tents. Large stones would be put in a circle in the middle of the tents, then an even bigger cast-iron stone would be placed at the bottom, surrounded by the outer stones. Once the firewood was burning, the glow and flickering that came from it reminded me of the candles that made the tents feel comfortable, even though they weren't.

The smoke from the fire would escape from the hole in the top of the tents, spiralling into the cold night air, then lots of straw would be spread around the tent floors, with old bedding on top of the straw to make it warm and comfortable for all to sleep on.

I loved the evening in the camp. With the big fires burning outside, everyone would sit around them talking about this and that. Drunken Father (that was my mother's name for him) would play his mouth organ, which he was brilliant at playing. We would watch his chubby cheeks as he blew air in and out of the object. Other members of the group would join in with their musical instruments, like the violin, spoons and the penny whistle. My mother, who had a voice like an angel, would sing old Irish folk songs in our native tongue of Gaelic. It was our first language and spoken by all. Cant was another language the Irish Traveller spoke. The country folk called it the tinker language or the secret language. It was always spoken within the Traveller community, especially when we went into the village or market and didn't want the Gorgie people to know what we were talking about.

My aunt Carrie, who had been to England a few times with her buck-toothed husband, would tell us grizzly stories about baby cows born with two heads and great big snakes with eight legs and other freakish things that she had seen and heard about while she was there.

"Mother of God!" Aunt June would cry. "Don't be telling us things like that. You'll put the fear of God into the children's minds."

The men from the camps sat separate from the women. It was the done thing and still is. They had their own fires and bundles of straw to sit on and the dark stuff to drink; and could they drink. Before long, men and women would be paralytic drunk, dancing and singing, their troubles forgotten for another day. Drunken Father would become argumentative with Mother until Uncle Oliver stopped him. We all loved Uncle Oliver, especially the children. He would play his penny whistle and all the little ones would dance around him barefoot. Not because they liked to jig around barefoot but because none of them had shoes to wear. I was the lucky one who did because he bought them for me.

Who's My Daddy?

There was speculation and rumours that Oliver was my real father. If it was true, then that explains why my drunken father, who I believed was my daddy, never spoke nicely or ever looked me in the face when I tried to talk to him until I was nine years old, and by then I believed he hated me completely.

My uncle Oliver always came looking for his family when he was on leave from the Irish Army. He was one of Drunken Father's younger brothers and very well-loved by all the women. He only had to flash his saucy smile at some of the girls who lived in the village and the camps. They would run off laughing like hyenas but keep looking back and waving their hands at him. He was six feet tall, with jet black wavy hair and beautifully-shaped white teeth. He was nicknamed 'the gentleman' amongst Travellers because he was always well-dressed and smart. Every town and village he travelled through he left a lot of broken hearts. Aunt Rose said he was the spitting image of Clark Gable without the moustache. I didn't know who that was because he didn't live in our camp.

My aunt Mary Helen sometimes would tease Mother, saying how the feck did she end up with 'The Drunk' and not Oliver. After all, she was going out with him before she met 'The Drunk'.

"What happened to ye?" she asked Mother, but Mother wouldn't oblige her with an answer.

All she would say was, "Not in front of the children, please." Aunty would carry on regardless.

"Look, Betty –" mother's real name – "if you don't love Oliver, give him back his heart and let move on with his life. He could be Bridie's dad – everyone has a conclusion to that. He makes it pretty obvious. She's the only child he brings presents, and why would any man do that?"

"No matter," Mother would say.

I didn't understand what was being said. I was just happy seeing him and very excited about the gift he bought for me only. I was special to him and he to me.

It didn't bother Drunken Father that his brother was looking out for me and would buy me winter coats, boots and a large shawl to wrap around my head. As far as he was concerned, he didn't have to worry over me or provide for me. If that's what Oliver wanted to do, so be it.

My drunken father's name was John Paul Doyle. He was a tinsmith by trade. If he wasn't in the pubs, he'd be roaming around wasteland and rubbish dumps with his old pony and cart looking for scrap metal. With some of the old metal he had collected, he'd make tin buckets and sell them around the houses or in the markets. If he was fortunate enough to find or be given old silver spoons, he would make pretty rings with them and sell them on to other Travellers for their women, plus he was quite an expert at manufacturing his very own half-crowns and took great delight spending them in a pub or two, knowing that they were so good and that he had fooled a lot of landlords with them.

He married my mother Betty Dublin in 1942 and fourteen years later I was born in a tent in Clairs Road, Moate, near Westmeath in Southern Ireland. They had to move onto the muddy field because Mother had been in labour for two days and needed to get off the road to give birth to me. She called me after her younger sister, Bridie, who had died of cancer in her bones at the age of fourteen. My aunty Mary Helen helped bring me into the world.

Mother's family was very poor. They sometimes worked in the convents and churches, scrubbing floors and doing other general domestic chores for a few pennies a week.

The priest and nuns used the Travellers for cheap labour, because they knew no one else would employ them because they were Travellers. By the time I was born, Mother had seven other children. If the other three children had lived, there would have been ten of us. She was only thirty years old.

Jeremy was the eldest. His twin died of convulsion fits and swallowed his tongue aged six months. My sister, Libby, was the eldest daughter, then Ocean and Kelly, and Brother Peter, and the two other babies who were stillborn, plus the miscarriage she had when she was two months gone, and then me.

My mother and her family were devoted Catholics, and it was her job, as far as she was concerned, to go forth and multiply. She was from a family of seven brothers and three sisters, plus one stepsister and two stepbrothers. Her mother had died when she was twelve years old, and her father soon remarried. My mother never spoke about her stepbrothers and stepsisters. She wouldn't accept them as any part of her family, hence why I never met them or my grandfather. She had met my drunken father at the age of sixteen, got married, and continued to have child after child. She never showed any affection to her daughters – only her sons got all the hugs and cuddles – but this didn't bother me because I was smothered with kisses and cuddles from my aunt Mary Helen. Drunken Father was just as bad. He didn't have time for any of his children, and half of the time you'd be lucky if he remembered your name, but they were my parents, and I loved them both.

With so many kids, my mother never knew from one day to the next where the next meal for them was coming from. She would spend hours out begging on the streets for money or food. Sometimes she would be lucky enough to earn half-a-crown telling the country folks their fortunes. Other times she would take my sister Ocean out begging with her because some people would take pity on Ocean. She had to wear callipers on her skinny legs due to rickets. Mother would say thank God he gave her Ocean with the gammy legs because, without her, the rest of the family would have starved with the hunger. I don't think poor Ocean looked at it that way.

I hated the winter months on the road, especially when it snowed. It seemed to last forever. All the wagons and tents would be covered in thick white snow. Even the poor dogs would vanish under it, as they weren't allowed inside the wagon or the tents. The only things that still moved around in the camps were the half-frozen women, who still had to go out begging.

The men couldn't go out looking for work because it was too dangerous to take the horses and carts on the roads.

I would watch my mother and some of my aunties doing their best, trying not to get their heavy black skirts wet in the snow. They'd lift them right up over their knees. I would giggle to myself at seeing my auntie's legs, knowing it was forbidden for the women to show their legs. As they moved slowly out of the camp, they didn't look like people anymore, just shadows trying not to trip over in the soft snow.

Once my mother had disappeared out of sight, Drunken Father would make haste. He'd be out of the wagon door like a long dog to see the woman he was having an affair with behind my mother's back. Well, I say behind her back, but she knew about it and chose to ignore it. The children would be left for hours in the cold tents to amuse themselves. The icy wind would blow into the tents and bite into their skin, and the cold would make their feet swell up. I was lucky. I had the warm boots that my uncle Oliver had bought for me, but my legs and hands were blue with the freezing weather.

Oh God, it was always a great relief to see Mother walking into the camp with armfuls of sticks and twigs and her big black shawl tied to her back filled with goodies. She and my auntie would get the fires going inside the tents, then they'd put the black pots that the children had filled up with snow on the fires. Once the snow had melted, Mother would pour the warm water over our hands and feet to get heat into them. The pain was excruciating, but after a while, it would wear off. All the food they had got would be shared out with everyone in the camp.

Once the children's bellies were filled, and they had been put to bed, Mother would say: "What is God to us?" And we all had to reply, "Good."

Baby Paul

I had a new member to my family. Drunken Father had given my mother another son who she called Paul Roy. I was no longer allowed to sleep in my aunt Mary Helen's tent because she'd had another of her rows with him for the way he was treating my mother. He was always beating up on my mother, and my aunt had had enough of his behaviour. So for pure spite, he laid down the law that I was forbidden to sleep in her tent again, but because I was the youngest child at that time, I soon got used to the comfort of sleeping next to my mother's warm body and the sounds of my Drunken Father's snoring and farting all night long. Now Paul Roy had the privilege of sleeping with her, and I was kicked out to the tent with my other siblings. I cried every night, hoping that my parents would take pity on me and let me go to my aunt's tent, but they were having none of it. My mother would say, "You got your big sisters to look after you," and suggested I should stop all the whingeing.

I didn't. Night after night I would be hollering like the old banshee for my auntie until one night Drunken Father was so fed up with me disturbing his sleep, he dragged me from the tent by my hair – well, what little hair I had – over the muddy field to where his big grey horse Billy was chained up.

"Do you see Billy's fat hairy arsehole? That's where I'm going to fecking shove you if you fecking get me up again. Now, what is it to be? The tents or up his arse?"

After that, I never cried out for my aunt or mother again.

A few weeks down the road, Drunken Father had gone missing again. This time for two weeks. Like I said, Mother knew he was seeing the 'other' woman, but she was frightened to confront him, just in case he would leave her for good. Aunt June was trying her best to explain to her that the fecker was no good for King or country, let alone her, but Mother was having none of her talk. She told everyone in the camp that she loved my drunken father, and she was willing to turn a blind eye to anything that he did or said to her because deep down in his heart he loved her as well.

Aunt Rose told her she was living in a daydream and needed to get her fucking head seen to. My mother always had excuses why she shouldn't leave him. Where could she go? What other men would take her on with her army of kids? And wasn't she damaged goods? And the thoughts about actually losing him and not sharing her life with him would send her into some madhouse. "What would happen to my children?" Mother would say, crying.

My aunt Mary Helen would always reassure my mother that she would stand by her whatever her decision, maybe even though she may not like it. She said she felt sorry for my mother, and the dark clouds that were moving over her head would always be there, looming, promising very bad things to come, until she got rid of that dirty bastard.

Mother, still crying, said she didn't need anyone feeling sorry for her. She felt sorry enough for herself, and that was the end of the matter. No more would be said about her alcoholic, unfaithful husband.

For the next three months, my family was pushed from pillar to post by the police. Within that short space of time, we had been kicked off twenty-eight illegal camps. For a few days, my family moved to Belfast, then Derry and Omagh, then back into the South of Ireland. We had a week in Waterford, a few more in Limerick, and then to Moate. One muddy field to another. All the time we were forced to move, my baby brother, Paul Roy, was sick. My mother put it down to him teething and, in the meantime, managed to find an emergency doctor to see Paul Roy. She was told not to worry, he was okay and she was given some medicine for his gums and told to bring him back to the doctors in a few days, just to keep an eye on him.

Mother didn't go back with him to the doctors because the council and police had once again moved my family on.

Drunken Father decided to move his family into the woods. He said it would be a safe place for a time, plus the weather was warm, and the grass would be dry, so there'd be no need for the children to be stuck in the tents all day getting bored out of their brains.

Mother agreed but hated the idea that they had to hide in the woods like wild animals just to keep the country folks happy.

Drunken Father said that sometimes out of sight, out of mind is a good thing, and he was right. We had four glorious months there. We were left alone from the police and the Gorgie lot. No torches flashing in the wagons' windows, no screaming children being dragged out of the tents by the police, and best of all, no mud. Mother may have disliked living there, but I loved it. To be able to run free all day long, pick bluebells and other wildflowers and hunt the leprechauns was just pure magic to me. Aunt Kathleen believed that little people were very lucky, and if you were fortunate enough to catch one, you would be granted a wish. Well, I know what my wish would be for Paul Roy to get better and then I could play with him. As it was, I was not allowed to pick him up, but it didn't stop me from trying.

Mother was always yelling, "Bridie! Will you fucking let that child be? He is too delicate for you to keep messing about with him. Once he is big and strong, then and only then you can play with him. Do you understand me?"

Paul Roy was ten months old and couldn't sit up or crawl like Aunt June's little fella. They were the same age, but Ben was a very lively child, and always up to some kind of mischief. Once, he crawled under one of the wagons, and poor Aunt June was frantic with worry. It took her a good hour pleading with him to crawl back out to her. It must have been hard for Mother seeing all the young babies in the camp doing so well and hers doing nothing. Sometimes, she only had to pick him up from his crib, and he would scream and cry as if he was in pain. Other times he would be staring into space and when you talked to him, he gave you no eye contact whatsoever. Mother rushed him back to the hospital, only to be told that all babies get poorly when their teeth are coming through, but somehow she knew that there was something seriously wrong with her son.

The next morning she was back at the hospital again. Paul Roy was burning up with a high fever and, once again, she was sent home with medication to bring down his fever. Aunt Mary Helen couldn't understand why the hospital didn't keep him in overnight.

"Obviously there's more to his illness. Why can't the divvy doctors see that?" she said to my mother.

"No matter, the medicine may help him," Mother replied.

The next morning, Mother ran out of the wagon, screaming with my little baby brother dead in her arms. All the women in the camp rushed over to her. Drunken Father sat on the steps of the wagon with his head in his hands, crying. I knew something bad had happened because I had never seen him crying before but didn't understand why the police had taken my parents and baby Paul Roy away with them.

I had never heard the word 'dead' before and didn't know the meaning of it. There was no one in the camp to explain what had occurred. All the adults had harnessed up their horses and carts and followed the police cars wherever they were going.

Late in the evening, the police returned without baby Paul Roy.

I asked my aunt Rose where my little brother was. "He's gone to Heaven," she replied.

"How far is that, and why is everybody crying, and when will my brother be coming home?"

"Will you stop fecking asking questions?" my aunt shouted at me. "Now be a good girl and go to bed."

Within days, my family's relations came to be with my parents. They came from all over Ireland, England, and America. Some brought their wagons, others came with tents, a lot of them for the six-day wake. It wasn't long before the police were getting complaints about the racket that was going on in the woods. The police kept well away from our camp because they had been informed about my brother's death and didn't see any point in aggravating the situation as everyone was on tenterhooks as it was. Best let us bury the dead and then move us on.

Music played day and night to celebrate the short life of my brother. It's a traditional thing. Your heart may be broken because of your loss and emotional pain, but there is a joy as well because God gave us you, but, unfortunately, I didn't get enough time to be with him.

For the next six days, people got drunk and cried for Paul Roy, mainly the men. The women were kept busy making the sandwiches and making pots of tea for the ones that didn't drink. There were about a hundred or more guests, plus the children had to be looked after as well. The adults didn't sleep until the wake was over; only the children had the privilege of sleeping. Four days later, the ambulance men brought back Paul Roy's little body to my family. He was put in the wagon that belonged to my parents, which had been done out with beautiful paper flowers that the women had made. His rocking crib was covered with white silk. Mother took him out of the small coffin because she said he didn't look like her baby in it and placed him in his crib for the last time. For the first time, I was allowed to kiss his forehead without Mother moaning at me. I still didn't realise it would be the last time I would see him again. To me, he was only asleep.

That night around the campfire, my aunt Mary Helen was telling all the other women about me putting black boot polish all over Paul Roy's head to make it look like his hair was growing. All the women laughed, except Mother. I think she was in a different world. She didn't speak, just stared into the fire, lost in her own thoughts.

Once he was buried, it was time to move on again. The wagon that Paul Roy had slept in and all his clothes were set on fire, so he would always have somewhere to live when in the next world.

We moved away to Cork after that because Mother didn't want to stay in Moate anymore. Even birds singing in the woods reminded her of Paul Roy. We were in Cork for seven months, and Mother found out she was with child again. Aunt Rose said God was good because he was giving her another child to take the pain away from her heart and fill her arms once again. Not to replace Paul Roy, but to make her whole again. Everyone was happy, even Drunken Father, who hadn't done one of his disappearing acts for some time, was delighted with the prospect of another child to add to his already large family, but Mother was apprehensive about the newcomer. She couldn't sleep, worrying that her new baby would have the same dreadful leukaemia disease that took baby Paul Roy's life. If only the doctors had listened to her, the symptoms that he was suffering with that she would tell the hospital about. She would say he did have very pale skin and had very high fevers and infections, one after the other. Maybe he could have been saved. Who knows?

The Burning of the Tent

It was a lovely evening. The sun was going down in a blaze of glory. I lay at the entrance of our tent, looking at the thin blue wisp of woodsmoke from the outside fire winding its way upwards through the silver birch trees. A blackbird was singing his little heart out on top of a twig of a hawthorn bush. A few wild rabbits were skipping and jumping around our tents.

They seemed to know that our dogs were tied up for the night and that they had the freedom to eat the luscious green grass to their hearts' content without getting themselves eaten by the dogs.

I may have only been four years old, but I just loved nature all around me. The beauty of the sky, the colour of the wildflowers, especially buttercups. It was said that if you put one under your chin and it is yellow, you like butter. Whether this is true or not, I don't know.

I fell asleep a happy little girl, knowing the sorrow and unhappiness had lifted from my family because they knew about the new baby coming, which was very gladly welcomed.

Suddenly, I was having a bad dream. I couldn't breathe. I could hear sounds of something crackling all around me, but couldn't see what was making the noise because foggy smoke was blinding my view. Voices were screaming, 'Get her out!' I realised it wasn't a dream when I felt someone pulling at my legs and trying to drag me away from the burning tent. That's all I could remember, until I woke up screaming for my aunt Mary Helen. She was nowhere in sight, neither were our wagons or tents, and all my family had disappeared.

I was lying in a bed, a real one at that, with sheets that were white as the clouds in the sky. A very old nun with a crooked smile on her face was saying, "Time to get up, tinker child." I thought to myself, *If I go back to sleep everything would be back to normal once again and when I wake I would be back in my tent snuggled up warmly next to my siblings*, but I couldn't go back to sleep, so I put my hands over my eyes and began to recite the Lord's Prayer in Gaelic: *Ar nAthair a tha air neamh,, gu naomhaichear d'ainm, Thigeadh do riochachd.*

I peeped through the gaps in my fingers, hoping my prayers were answered. They were not. The nun was still there hovering over me like the Devil himself.

"When you have finished playing peekaboo, I suggest you sit up," she said. She reached out to grab my arm, and I did what I could do the best, scream my lungs out. I always did that when I felt under threat, and my aunt Mary Helen would usually come running to my rescue and yell at whoever was bullying me. I waited for her quick arrival to come to my aid, but there was no sign of her. I caused such a stink, which brought a lot of other nuns running into the dormitory.

"Look what the little cow has done...only bit my arm!" cried Sister Mary with the crooked smile, who was holding onto my arm while Sister Teresa was holding onto my hair.

"Let her hair go, Sister Teresa. Can't you see she is terrified?" As she sat on the bed next to me, the nun speaking these words said her name was Sister Bernadette. She tried to explain to me in her soft voice that I would be staying in the orphanage for a while and that I would see my family very soon. For some unknown reason, I felt a connection between us.

I said I didn't want to stay with her and the nun that pulled my hair. "When my auntie Mary Helen finds out she done that to me, she will kick her fecking arse, so best she takes me home before they all get their asses kicked in."

Sister Bernadette laughed at me and said it looked like she was going to have to take me under her wing. She told me our tent had burnt down and me and my siblings were very lucky to be alive and unhurt. If it wasn't for the policeman that pulled me out, only the Good Lord knows what would have happened to us all.

The local newspaper article read:

Tyrrellspass Garda's Plucky Action.

Nine children named Rattigan living in a camp near Newtown, Tyrrellspass, County Westmeath escaped serious injury when a spark set fire to their roadside tent. They were taken to safety by Garda Brendan Sheehan, Tyrrellspass, who was on duty in the vicinity. Garda Sheehan received burns on his neck. Both the children's father, a labourer employed by the Westmeath Co. Council, and their mother were absent at the time of the occurrence.

"Well," said Sister Bernadette, "I will be the one who be looking after you from now on, so stop crying, child, and come with me."

I held her hand as she took me downstairs and into a very large room, known as the dining room. There were tables and chairs dotted all over the place. At the top end of the room, there were two tables on each side, where four nuns sat at each table, eating.

I was left in the care of Sister Teresa, who introduced me to the other children, saying,

"This is Bridget."

"No, it's not. I am called Bridie," I said boldly.

"Bridie is short for Bridget, you stupid girl." Sister Teresa continued to tell the children how fortunate I was to be given the name of a great saint who healed the sick.

"Of course," I piped up again, telling everyone who was interested.

Not that the children looked up or cared who I was called after. The only interest they had was to get back to eating their bread and jam.

"I'm not called after what's-her-face. My drunken father named me after his old donkey, who died. He said so," I proudly said.

"I see we will have to teach you some manners," Sister Teresa replied with gritted teeth.

For months on end, I walked around the home like a lost child, crying day and night for my aunty. Surprisingly, I never shed a tear for my mother or drunken father, or siblings, come to that. I stood looking out of the big bay window that had the view to the convent entrance expecting to see Aunty Mary Helen coming to rescue me from the loneliness and confusion that were eating me up.

I asked Sister Teresa why my aunt didn't come for me. Her reply was very cruel: "Your family doesn't want you; hence that's why you are here with us. Your mother handed you over to the Sisters of Mercy. You should thank your lucky stars that we were willing to give you a home, my girl. Now go and play with the other children, you can't stay glued to the window."

I carried on staring out of the window.

"The choice is yours."

Secret Garden

A year had passed, and I realised no one was coming for me. I was devastated to think I might never see any of my family again. I had no friends in the home and distrusted everyone. Some of the nuns were very unfriendly and obviously didn't like me because of my temperament, which was up and down from one day to the next. I didn't know how to make friends or even if I could trust anyone to be my friend. I woke up every day feeling sad and helpless and hurting and confused. If I had my way, I would have been quite happy to stay in bed all day with my misery, but Sister Teresa was having none of it. Every morning she'd be hovering over my bed like a fly.

"Up you get, tinker child. God waits for no one," she'd say as she dragged the bed covers from me. She'd be livid once she realised I'd wet the bed again. A smack across the face soon woke me up, but I was hardened to her ways by now and wouldn't give her the satisfaction of her seeing me crying. She decided to put a pisspot under my bed and gave strict instructions to "use it or else". I was too frightened to get out of bed in the pitch-dark dormitory, so I continued to wet the bed.

An epidemic of measles broke out in the home. The nuns didn't know if I was vaccinated against the disease, so it was decided I should be vaccinated just in case I hadn't. I had a bad reaction to the injection and was rushed to the hospital, which was located on the convent grounds. I drifted in and out of consciousness for a few days. My body was covered with a red rash and the vomiting never seemed to stop. I didn't know at that time that the doctors and nurses were struggling to save my life.

I remember having psychic dreams. I could see myself walking in this beautiful garden. The garden was so big it seemed to go on for miles and miles. There were all kinds of animals roaming the grounds which I'd never seen before. They paid no attention to me. I had no fear of them; neither did any of the children who seemed to be playing with them. A young boy with olive skin who said his name was Isaac asked if I would like to come and play with him and the others. I began chasing after him. The sun was shining so bright it filled me with energy and love, then I heard a female voice singing so soft and sweet. I instantly recognised the song. It was the Irish lullaby that my aunt

Mary Helen used to sing all the time. I don't think I'd ever felt so happy at that moment in time, knowing and believing that my auntie hadn't rejected me like Sister Teresa had said. I began running towards the voice as if my whole life depended on reaching the singer.

I opened my eyes, and to my horror, it was Sister Bernadette, who was singing, not my auntie. Everything was such a blur, and I couldn't understand why I was lying in bed with tubes coming out of every part of my body and needles in both of my arms. Sister Bernadette was talking to me, but I couldn't make out what she was saying. Her voice seemed a long way away. I must have drifted back to sleep. Within no time, I was allowed to leave the hospital.

Sister Bernadette, for reasons of her own, took me under her wing. I began to feel secure and safe for the first time in a long time. She became my mother and family all in one. With her help and love, I soon adjusted to the home, but not all their rules.

The orphanage had its own school, laundry, and hospital within the grounds. There were over a hundred nuns to look after us kids, ranging from eighteen months to seventeen years old. The older girls in the home attended school lessons in the mornings and worked in the laundry in the afternoons. They were kept separate from the younger children. Why this was, I didn't know. The school had eight classrooms and rows of toilets and a small cloakroom.

I hated going to school. It was so boring. Sister Teresa was my form teacher. She felt it wasn't necessary to teach us to read and write. She was only interested in teaching us about God, Jesus and Mary, and how God was going to punish us because we were naughty children, especially the ones who pissed the bed. Of course, when she was saying this, she was looking straight at me, the old cow. I swear she made her own commandments up as she went along: thou shalt not suck thy thumb; thou shalt not leave food on the plate when there are so many starving children in the world. I would tell her the hungry kids could have my food, especially the meat, which I refused to eat every day. It was always chicken. I had it in my head that the nuns, for pure badness, had slaughtered all my pet chickens and were trying to force me to eat them because I wouldn't obey their silly rules.

So, I was going to burn in Hell because I wasn't a good Catholic child. It didn't bother me, so I didn't see why they were ripping their hair out – that's if they had any hair under their habits – because I didn't believe in Jesus or any of their other saints, or Father Christmas, come to that. I'd never had a present from him, the tight git.

As time passed, I became cunning to their ways. I realised, if I didn't call Sister Teresa feckface or tell her she was a big fat lesbian, she'd allow me out in the convent grounds by myself. There were acres of it, but I had to keep within the boundary of the church for the time being. The chapel was a huge old building. I loved the collection of old books, which were full of beautiful pictures of the previous owner's wife and kids, and others of Moses and King Solomon. There was a sweet smell of incense that made you want to cough your stomach up. On the altar was a very large statue of Jesus with long blonde hair and blue eyes. Considering he was supposed to have been born in Bethlehem, why didn't he have olive skin, black hair and dark eyes like all the people in the picture books? Under the statue, several little candles flickered, sending shadows darting along the floor and up the white walls. There were rows of tiny benches for the children to sit on, plus larger ones for the nuns.

Two priests were in charge of the church. They wore long black dresses like nuns. Their deep voices confused me, so I asked Sister Bernadette one day if they were he-shes. The poor nun nearly had a heart attack and demanded to know who taught me such a word. "My aunt Mary Helen did," I told her proudly, and continued to say that my aunt Rose said there were people who had someone else living inside them. One day they'd be a girl, the next a boy. We had one that was allowed to come into our camps any time he or she liked. Our families adored him, just as he or she loved us. Sometimes, the he-she wore dresses and looked like a China doll, so my father said my uncle Oliver often said that he-she was better looking than some of the women in the camp, which upset a lot of them.

I asked Sister Bernadette why the priests wore long dresses if they were not he-shes, and whether they had a minny like me and her.

"God, my child, you do ask awkward questions for a four-year-old," came her reply. "No, men are different."

"How different?" I said.

"Shall we just say they've got deep voices and leave it at that?" said the old nun.

I was quite happy with her explanation of male and female genders and skipped off to play.

A few days later, I bumped into Father Daly in the convent grounds.

"Hello, Bridie. I see you are off on your wandering again. Do the sisters know you are out here?" he asked.

I completely ignored his question and told him I knew the difference between him and me. He went red as a red tomato in the face and began shouting that I was an evil child, and he was going to pray for my sick soul. He walked away from me in disgust and now and then looked back at me, shaking his head. I couldn't understand why he went off on one. I was only going to say our voices weren't the same. I shouted after him that he was an old fuckface, not that I knew what that meant; it was a word I'd heard so often in our camp. When the women had a disagreement with each other, one would say to the other, "Go away fuckface, or I beat the head off ya," and before you knew it, they'd be punching each other's heads in.

Once I was back indoors, I found the old priest had grassed me up to the Mother Superior. I was told I was going to be denied my supper for that evening. I threw a screaming tantrum, which I must say I was brilliant at. My grandma Betty, who was my father's mother, always said if you can't get what you want, throw a tantrum. It always worked out for me in the camps, but not with Sister Teresa, who I swear had no legs because she didn't walk like the other nuns, she floated. I nicknamed her Sister No Legs. She wasn't amused with her new name. Every time I called her that she would twist my ear, which was painful. By the time I left the orphanage, it looked like my right ear was deformed.

She would lock me in a dark room until my screaming fits stopped. I'd lay there in the dark, terrified. My imagination would run away with itself. I would think everything in the room was moving, even the darkness, not that I could see anything. Every now and then, I called out that I was sorry, hoping to get a response, but no one came back. When the door was finally opened, I would be found in a heap on the floor fast asleep.

"Now, will you promise you be a good girl from now on?" said Sister No Legs.

"I promise."

"That's a good girl."

But some promises are meant to be broken. Well, at least mine were. Once a week I would find myself being dragged into the dark room because I was naughty. It's no wonder why I was terrified of the dark, and still am today. I can't sleep without a light on or the TV, because I have bad nightmares or night terrors that scare the living daylights out of me. I know I didn't come in from the grounds when the nuns called me, but I didn't think that was naughty enough to be punished the way I was. I may have only been a four-year-old, but I know I wasn't really a bad child or the Devil's child, which I was so frequently called by Sister No Legs.

The all-girls' home, grounds and gardens were beautiful. A long drive led from the big oak front door to the high iron gates that were kept shut at all times to keep the children in and the rest of the outside world out. I would stand at the gates, watching and waiting for my aunt Mary Helen to appear. I suppose I knew after being in the orphanage for a year that she probably wouldn't be coming for me, but it didn't stop me looking out for her.

I loved playing out in the convent grounds on my own, chasing the wild rabbits, and climbing the highest trees to see if I could touch the sky. The higher I climbed, the further the sky seemed to be away from me.

The autumn months were my favourite. I would rustle barefoot through the fallen leaves, ankle-deep, and search through them for conkers. To me, they were shiny brown treasures in their spiky green cases. Once I had gathered them all up, I'd put them under the trees for the leprechauns so they could repair their homes with them. Sister Bernadette said some of the wild winds that came in off the coast damaged and flooded their houses, so they needed the conkers to block up the holes. The other nuns seemed to be quite happy with Sister Bernadette's plan to allow me the freedom of the grounds. All the time I was out there doing my good Samaritan deeds, I wasn't getting up to mischief elsewhere.

At the far end of the grounds was the convent kitchen where all the children's and nuns' food was prepared. It was strictly out of bounds to all the kids, except the older girls from the home who helped to prepare the meals. I had snuck in there many times to rob an apple or two. Next to that were the vegetable and fruit gardens, carefully tended to by the young nuns and novices, who hadn't yet taken up their vows to become a fully-fledged nun. Apple, pear and other fruit trees grew up against the kitchen walls. There were row after row of different vegetables growing, soft fruits and patches of herbs.

I sat high up in one of the big trees watching the nuns and novices with their sleeves rolled up, their faces hot and red under their headdresses, pulling up the cabbages for the day's dinner. I'd catch a glimpse of their black wellington boots under their heavy black habits, wishing I had wellies like them.

Mischievous Tinker Child

The years soon trickled by, and I reached the grand old age of seven. I was a constant source of irritation and aggravation to some of the sisters. I was always in trouble over something or other. I would spend hours roaming the grounds just to keep out of the way. There were other areas of the grounds I couldn't get into. It wasn't because the big iron gates were too high for me to climb – the pieces of glass that were attached to the tops looked deadly, and I didn't fancy ripping my hands to bits trying to get over them.

Sister Teresa, the nun with no legs, always came to find me. I could hear her angry voice, yelling, "Tinker's child, come here at once." You'd think after four years of being in the orphanage that she would have remembered my name. I knew she loathed me, like I disliked her intensely. I couldn't understand why she treated me so badly. If other kids hit me, I'd punch them back, but Sister No Legs would say it was my fault. She'd hit me with a ruler on my knuckles and hands, leaving them stinging for days. It didn't matter what I did, even if I was trying to be good, it was bad. In her eyes, the 'tinker's child' could never do anything right. As far as she was concerned, I gave up trying to please her because she was incapable of ever being pleased with me, so I focused more on getting my own back on her. It wasn't long before I put my plans into action.

One frosty morning, I had gone missing again from Sister No Legs' religious classes. I hated them. So God has rejected me because I was born a sinner, and I will be doomed to Hell to burn with Satan forever. For God to be my friend, I had to tell him every day I was sorry for disobeying him, for being stubborn and not doing what the nuns told me to do. Her complaints list about all my wrongs seemed to go on for eternity. As if I wasn't feeling guilty enough already, she had to keep pointing out how Jesus died for my sad sins.

I worked it out in my head: if I committed three sins a day, like wetting my bed, sucking my thumb, and back-chatting Sister No Legs, I had murdered God's son every day. I couldn't see how, considering I'd never met him. It was only a few weeks back that she'd said the Roman soldiers had killed Jesus. Now she was putting the blame on me.

Walking around the grounds that morning, I stumbled across a baby rabbit. It didn't move when I got close to it. I was going to pick it up, but I could see its mother and other little ones running around their nest. I decided to leave it be and come back later. When I did, it was dead. I was so upset I ran to Sister Bernadette's bedroom, sobbing my eyes out, trying to explain to her it wasn't my fault that the rabbit died. I felt so bad thinking that if I had picked it up, maybe it would still be alive. Sister Bernadette, who had been confined to her bed because she had a bad cough and troublesome back pain, had to wear a metal brace around her neck. She told me it was to stop her head from falling off.

She assured me that the death of the rabbit was down to nature. I stopped whingeing and ran as fast as my little legs would run and picked up the stiff rabbit and put it in Sister No Legs' bed. For the rest of the day, I walked around with a big smile on my face, knowing I hadn't murdered Jesus or the rabbit. Nature did it, whoever Nature was.

Sister No Legs didn't find the dead rabbit until the next morning, even though she slept in her bed that night.

"Who done this?" Her voice was almost a scream. I was dying to laugh but knew better. The rest of the children sat on their beds with frozen faces.

She knew it was me, but had no proof she came over to my bed, stripped back my bedding and said, "Look, children, Bridget has wet her bed again. Can anyone please tell me what happens when you wet the bed?"

"They get punished," said Mary McDonald with a big smirk on her face. She was Sister No Legs' pet and could never do any wrong in her eyes.

This really embarrassed me.

"Hold your hand out," said Sister Teresa, who had no legs.

I wouldn't because I knew she would put all her strength into her elbows. Instead, she whacked me across my legs with the ruler that she kept in her habit pocket for her to strike out at any time at a child who misbehaved.

I was at the point of crying but stopped myself. I had made a decision a long time back not to let her beat me down. I just wished my mummy, Sister Bernadette, would hurry up and get better. Once she was well enough, she would be allowed to resume her duties as the head sister of my dormitory again. She was a very good person with a good heart. Unlike Sister No Legs, who would make us clean up our own vomit if anyone sicked up. If I got frightened at night, which was very often, I could go to Sister Bernadette's bedroom, which the nuns called cells, and climb into her small bed. She'd put her long arms around me and say I had nothing to fear. I loved Sister Bernadette dearly and couldn't wait for her health to improve.

I woke up one night, busting for a wee. I got out of my bed and hopped into Mary McDonald's bed. Once I'd relieved my bladder, I got back into my own one, pleased with myself. I thought if it's a mortal sin to wet your bed, then let Mary McDonald be a sinner as well. Bet she won't find it funny seeing the other girls, including myself being punished again, because now she'll get what is coming to her, and I couldn't wait. The old witch did her morning rounds. She'd ring her bell to tell us to get up and stand at the side of our beds.

She'd walk to each bed in turn, strip back the bedding, and touch the sheets to see if they were wet. She came to my bed and nearly had a heart attack to find it dry.

"My, my," she said as she moved on to her favourite child's bed, which was next to mine.

"Good morning, Mary my dear. Did you sleep well?"

"Yes," said Mary, looking a bit stressed out.

It was not surprising Mary was Sister No Legs' pet, and some of the other nuns as well. She was so pretty, her blonde hair just hanging down in beautiful ringlets, with her baby-face and sparkling blue eyes, and the little birthmark on the side of her right cheek which looked like an angel wing. She was tall as a giraffe and had the biggest feet I'd ever seen on an eight-year-old girl. Was I jealous of beautiful Mary McDonald? Of course I was.

"Jesus, Mary, and Joseph! Your bed is soaking wet," said Sister No Legs.

Poor Mary's face went white as a ghost. Big tears ran down her face like raindrops. I did feel sorry for her for a moment, but it soon passed when Sister No Legs said, "There, my lovely, don't cry. Everyone is entitled to one mishap."

She cuddled Mary tightly in her arms. She never held me in her skinny arms, except when I swore at her. Then she shook me so hard even the lice in my hair would run for cover, thinking it was an earthquake.

Mary wasn't shamed in front of the other girls like I was hoping for. Instead, she was confined to bed. The elder girls had to make it up with clean sheets and bring all her meals to her while she was in bed, and she was given a raspberry lollipop – something I was never given.

I couldn't stop wetting the bed, no matter how hard I tried. I couldn't put up with being hit every morning with Sister No Legs' ruler until one morning she realised it had gone missing from her room. I took it, hoping now that she had nothing to hit us with she would stop, but not her. She began hitting us with her smelly old slippers. She wasn't amused when they disappeared as well.

She made us all swear on the Bible that we hadn't been in her room or taken her slippers. I kept my two fingers crossed behind my back as I took the oath. I lied.

I was dying to tell her that her belongings were up the big oak tree where I had hidden them, but thought better of it and kept quiet. I wasn't quite sure if God was going to forgive me for blatantly lying, but at least it stopped the bed-wetters, including myself, from being punished for quite some time.

A new nun took charge of our dormitory, and strangely enough, from the night she did, I stopped wetting the bed. Sister Madeleine put little pisspots under our beds, plus she left a dim light on in the bedroom, making it less frightening for us to get out of bed to use the potty. She was in charge of the six to nine-year-olds for about eleven months, before she was sent off to South Africa to help the starving children. I missed her dreadfully.

Sister Bernadette, my mummy, who I referred to as that from the age of four, had now left the orphanage hospital. She had been in there for some months now, suffering from something called 'to-burp-smoker-lotus'. It wasn't until later years that I realised the proper name was 'tuberculosis'.

Her new cell (room) was just down the corridor from my dormitory. I knew I was forbidden from going near her, but I needed to see her. Every day and night I would sneak into her cell without being seen. I had to sit in the corner of her tiny room because of her illness. I didn't care. All that mattered to me was being with her. She was dressed from head to toe in white, and every time I entered her cell, she'd put a white mask over her mouth and make me wear one too. The mask smelled horrible, like the disinfectant that the girls had to scrub the floors with. It made me feel sick, but I knew if I didn't keep it on, Mummy would get upset with me. She sent me out of her cell once because I took the mask off.

I would tell her about all the mischief I had been up to and how Sister No Legs was very angry with me.

"She *has* got legs, and why is she upset with you again?" Sister Bernadette asked.

"I did nothing," I replied.

"Nothing?"

"Well, I only stole a few of Nikki Smith's chocolates."

"How many was a few?" asked my mummy.

"The whole box, but it was only a little box," I replied. "I did ask her could I have one. She refused, even when I told her I'd never had a chocolate before, so I watched her hiding them under her pillow. I only meant to take one, but they were so yummy I couldn't stop eating them."

"Did you apologise to Nikki?" asked Mummy.

"No." But I said I would, just to please my mother.

I had no intention of saying I was sorry. After all, if she had let me have one in the first place, I wouldn't have taken them. It was her fault, as far as I was concerned, for being so greedy.

Forbidden Building

On another of my escape adventures from Sister No Legs, I had hidden myself away in my favourite place. The folly stood tall at the bottom of the convent grounds. It had a tiled roof and glass all the way around the building. Inside had benches around the walls. It was so peaceful just to sit there, away from all the hustle and bustle that went on inside the home.

One particular morning, I noticed a tall, skinny girl with black hair and wearing glasses. She was around fifteen or sixteen years old. I had not seen her before and wondered who she was.

"What's your name?" I asked her.

"I got no name," came her reply.

"Everyone got a name. Mine is Bridie. I was called after a donkey or saint, one or the other. It means 'shining bright'. My mummy, Sister Bernadette, said so."

The girl who had no name wasn't taking any notice of me. She seemed to be staring unseeingly into the distance as if she was expecting someone. Every now and then, she would sigh as if she was going to speak, but thought better of it.

Suddenly, I felt a bad feeling in the pit of my stomach that something really bad was going to happen, and I couldn't stop it. I took my eyes away from the strange girl for a second. That's when I heard the sound of breaking glass. The girl with no name was standing silently with both of her hands through the broken window. Blood was spurting like a water fountain from her wrists and running down her hands, covering her white apron and splashing onto the muddy floor. She showed no emotion, just stared emptily into the distance. Her pretty face was as white as a sheet. I ran to get help for her and bumped into Sister No Legs, who was out on her rounds looking for me. She floated off and was soon back with a handful of other nuns. I watched as Sister Jane pressed the girl's slashed wrists together and bound them tightly into a praying position. The nuns carried the poor girl into the hospital, with me following them. One of the nuns said as they entered inside that the girl had passed and may God and all the saints forgive her for the sin she had just committed.

I didn't understand what passing meant and asked Sister Rose if the girl's hands would get better. She screamed at me to get back to school at once.

I didn't. Instead, I ran to the big conker tree and climbed up it. From there, I could see all the comings and goings within the home's grounds. A group of girls who I didn't know was standing outside the folly. I could tell they were crying because they were wiping their eyes with handkerchiefs. They were all dressed the same: long-patterned dresses, knitted cardigans, long white socks and brown sandals.

One of the girls said they'd better get back to work. I watched them entering a building that I was forbidden to go near. It had never crossed my mind before to sneak into this house because it looked a cold and unfriendly place, but seeing the group of girls entering it got my curiosity running wild. I told myself, just a little peek wouldn't hurt anybody, and if I was quick enough, I could be in and out without anybody even knowing I was in there.

Inside, the forbidden building didn't look that much different from the house I lived in. The dining room furniture was large and dull and looked very old, like the room. The kitchen was spotlessly clean. The food larder was stuffed with all different types of food, and on top of the fourth shelf, just sitting there begging me to eat it, was the biggest chunk of chocolate gorking down on me. I managed to pull one of the large dining room chairs inside the larder. I reached up and grabbed a tray of eggs by mistake. The tray came tumbling down on top of my head. The eggs had smashed, sending their contents all over my head and running down my face. I wiped the gooey stuff away from my eyes and continued on my quest to get that chocolate if it killed me, as my mummy, Sister Bernadette, was always telling me, if I was after something good in my life, keep going until I got it. Sitting on the kitchen floor, with runny eggs all over me, I bit into the gigantic chocolate, only to realise I didn't like the fluffy jammy stuff inside it, but it didn't stop me filling my face with it. Once I'd had enough, I dragged the large chair to the sink, washed my face and hands to get rid of all the evidence, just in case I got caught, and then continued on my journey around the house.

The dormitories were very long and seemed to have hundreds of beds on each side of the walls.

On one of the big beds lay a baby propped up against the pillar. I went over and said hello to it. She was dressed all in pink and even wore pink shoes. Her long brown hair was plaited and tied at the bottom with ribbons. Her brown eyes peeped at me, but didn't move. I picked her up to give her a cuddle. She felt all rubbery and dangled from my arms. I threw her back on the bed and that's when she cried, "Mama."

I could hear footsteps along the corridor and hid under one of the beds.

"Norah, what happened to your doll?"

Oh please, God, don't let them find me, I prayed. *I didn't mean to kill her baby doll.*

"Look, Joan, it's got bits of eggshell on it. I bet it was that feckin' Alice who done this, to get her own back on me," said Norah.

"I'll feckin' kill her, you wait and see," replied Joan.

Oh dear, sounds like poor Alice is going to get a good hiding, all because of me. I didn't know the stupid thing was a doll. I'd never seen one in my life before and couldn't forewarn Alice; I didn't know her.

I stayed under the bed until I felt safe enough to come out.

I ran down the stairs with my heart pumping out of my mouth into a backyard that I didn't recognise. I tried to rack my seven-year-old brain as to where I'd gone wrong, but somehow it wasn't connecting with me. I couldn't climb the high walls that enclosed the yard, so, seeing a smaller red brick building, I hurried through the door, only to end up in a room that was full of all different kinds of machines. The girls I had seen at the folly were scrubbing clothes in large sinks. Others were putting sheets through a machine, only for them to come out the other side crisp and dry. Others were ironing.

"Well, well. What have we got here?" said one of the girls, coming towards me.

"I got myself lost," I said.

All the other girls laughed, except the nun who was sitting watching over the girls working.

"Get back to your work," she yelled at them, then pointed her finger at me to come over to her.

I was too scared to move. I had it in my mind to run, but there was nowhere to run to.

Another nun came into the laundry and grabbed me by my ear. "Don't you know this place is out of bounds to you, you little devil?" she said.

"Let go of me, you old witch!" I said as I was struggling to get away from her.

"Jesus, Sister, did you hear what she just called me, the little bitch?"

By now, all the girls were screaming at the nun not to hurt me. One of them said she would take me back to the children's house if she was permitted. A hard slap across the girl's face gave her the answer – no.

I kept kicking at the nun's legs, hoping she would let go of my hair. She was pulling at it with all her might as she was dragging me out of the room. I swear she was trying to scalp me.

Mother Superior wasn't amused as the old witchy nun told her lies about me. "What's that mess in your hair and on your frock?" Mother Superior demanded to know.

I had forgotten about the eggs and had to think of something really quickly.

"It's blood. She did that to me," I said and pretended to cry.

"Blood is red, as you are well aware, Bridie. That muck on your clothing is yellow and looks like dried eggs."

"Oh that," I said. "A big bird egg fell on me when I was standing underneath a tree."

"Was it a very big bird?" asked Mother Superior.

"It was gigantic, with big fat feathers, and its head was nearly as big as mine."

I think I won the old dragon over because she had a wide smile on her face. For the four years, I had been in the home, I had never seen a smile on her wrinkly face before.

I was handed over to Sister No Legs to be washed and changed. As always she took the greatest delight in dishing out my punishment.

It didn't bother me being locked in the dark room anymore. I'd sussed it out. All I had to do was pull one of the chairs to the large window and pull back the big wooden shutter to let the light in. As soon as I heard footsteps coming up the hallway, I'd close up the shutter, put the chair back where I'd got it from, and pretend I was asleep.

The punishment room was quite large. In one of the corners were lots of statues of Jesus, Mary, Joseph and others. I've no idea who they were. All of them were damaged in some way: heads, arms, legs missing. Hanging upon the walls were the outfits that the priests would wear for Sunday Mass. On top of the table were lots of boxes that I'd never seen before. Opening one of the boxes, I took out a bottle that I thought had red juice in. I opened the bottle, smelled it, and drank some of it. It was really nice, so I decided to have another sip and then another.

By the time Sister No Legs came to fetch me, I was sweating all over the place. My head was pumping, and my stomach felt very sick. I was put to bed, and the doctor called in to see me. She told the nuns to keep giving me warm salty water to drink. She wanted to know where I had got the wine from. Sister Jane explained that the wine had only been delivered the day before and was kept locked away from the children, but for some unknown reason, it was put in the punishment room.

"Punishment room? What happens in there?" asked the doctor.

"It's only used for the children who rebel against the rules," said Sister No Legs.

"They're only kept in the dark for an hour then released. The majority of the children never have to go back in the room," piped up Sister Margaret.

I gave the doctor one of my pitiful looks, hoping she would tell the witchy nuns off for putting me in the punishing room in the first place. All she said was to make sure they put the wine in a safer place in the future. I could have vomited in the piss pot that one of the nuns gave to me but, instead, I decided to puke up all over the doctor's white starched apron and on her black habit. The smell of my sick was putrid. It made me throw up again, this time all over Sister No Legs.

I may have felt like I was dying, but at least I would go with a smile on my face, knowing I had got my own back on them.

Mummy's Gone to Heaven

My mummy was dying, not that I understood what that meant. She was going to meet Jesus soon, because he had a lot of other children for her to look after. Somehow I had the notion I was going with her to the new orphanage. I presumed that's where Jesus was taking her, and there was no way he would expect her to leave me behind, would he?

I hadn't seen her for a couple of days because the nuns were in and out of her room, tending to her needs and praying for her. It was impossible for me to get a look-in because I was still banned from entering her room. Late one night, I woke up with an urgency I had to go to my mummy, Sister Bernadette. I made my way down the long, dark corridor towards her room. I had to stop now and then because the wooden floorboards would creak, and I was expecting one of the nuns whose rooms were on the same landing to jump out on me from the shadows. I crept as quietly as possible, like a thief in the night, until I reached her room.

"I have been waiting for you, my child," Mummy said as I climbed into her bed next to her, once I had put on the white mask that was identical to the one she was wearing. I was able to give her cuddles. I loved the feeling of her arms around me. It made me feel secure and safe and wanted. Mummy seemed to have lost weight, and I was frightened to hold her too tightly in case I broke her bones or injured her in some way. Her voice was so soft; it was difficult to understand what she was saying at times. I had to keep putting my ear to her mouth. I promised her I would behave myself and keep out of trouble so that the Mother Superior wouldn't have any excuses not to allow me to go to the new orphanage with her, but, knowing that old battle-axe, she'd find some excuse or other just to keep me here, I said.

Mummy laughed, then asked me to open the window, saying the room was a bit stuffy.

The night air was fresh, and the sky was full of stars. I got so excited seeing a shooting star racing across the sky as if it was in a hurry to get wherever it was going.

I turned to tell Mummy, but I assumed she had gone to sleep because she was making a snoring noise, which was unusual. I had slept in her bed many times and had never heard her snore.

I woke up sometime later. The room was freezing. I closed the window and went back to my dormitory to fetch my blanket. Mummy was still asleep when I climbed back into her bed again but was no longer snoring. She was very cold to the touch, so I covered her with my bedding and cuddled up to her.

Mother Superior woke me up. She had a look of horror on her face.

I'm in for it now, I thought. *Back to the punishing room for me.*

I had a quick glance back at Mummy as two nuns appeared out of nowhere and dragged me out of the room. She was still sound asleep, so I shouted out loud that I would see her later.

It was announced to me at that time that my mummy had died during the night. All the while I thought she was sleeping, she was dead.

I wasn't sent to the punishing room but was confined to bed instead and given a small white pill to take, and that's all I remember. How long I slept and was given the little white pills, I can't recall. I felt like I was drifting in and out of another world. I had no fear in the other world because my mummy was there with me. I could see children running through green meadows barefoot, trampling down the wildflowers that were growing under their feet.

I presumed we were at the other orphanage, but how we got there, I had no idea. The landscape seemed to run for miles and miles and the waterfalls seemed to have rainbows darting in and out of them. *God,* I thought, *this place is just beautiful. Better than the old dumpy orphanage I've left behind.*

I could hear the voice again. "Wake up, Bridie, come on."

I opened my eyes to find Sister No Legs hovering near me. "Come on, girl, you need a bath. Your body odour is disgusting."

I must admit I felt a lot better once washed and put into a clean nightdress. I wasn't allowed downstairs with the other children until I was completely well. I told Sister No Legs I wasn't sick, but for some unknown reason to me, she seemed to believe I was. Back in bed, I was given a big bowl of home-made leek and potato soup, crusty bread, and to my surprise, a raspberry lollipop, then another white pill, and in no time I was back in the land of dreams once again.

One morning, I rushed to my mummy's bedroom and banged on the door. I expected to hear her say, "Come in, Bridie." Nothing.

I presumed she was still asleep, so I knocked louder. Still no answer. I tried to open the door – it was locked. I felt panic inside my stomach. She never locked her room. I knew she wasn't well enough to be up to doing her duties, so why not open her door to me? I didn't believe she had gone away from me.

"Stop that noise, do you hear me?" said Sister Mary, waving her bony finger at me.

"What do you think you are playing at? Why are you knocking at the door?" yelled Sister June.

"I want my mummy," I cried.

"How many times do we have to tell you? She is with Jesus and all the saints in Heaven."

I was very confused. Wasn't I with her last night, running around the green meadows with her and a lot of children as she looked on?

"Sister Bernadette is dead. Now that's that."

How I cried as I felt a cold hand of fear tighten its grip on my chest. "Why are you all lying to me? I hate you all," I yelled.

Sister No Legs, who seemed to hover in mid-air, tried to grab my arm to give me an injection. I told her under no circumstances was she sticking that in my arm. "I'll put that up your arse first."

"The child is demented. A few days' punishment in the bad room will cure her sick mind," said Sister No Legs.

"Come with me, Bridie," said Sister Mary. "I promise no more needles, so stop crying like a good girl."

I'd been so out of it, I hadn't even realised I'd had any needles.

I followed Sister Mary back to my dormitory like a lost lamb. She sat on my bed and was trying to explain that I was only having dreams of Sister Bernadette, and what I was seeing wasn't real. She said lots of people imagine strange things when they lose a loved one. I didn't understand what she was saying.

"How can my mummy get lost when she never left her bedroom?" I asked.

"I mean, she's lost to you and us. God has taken her to Heaven with him and she is not in pain anymore."

"Why didn't she take me with her?" I asked.

"Because she's dead, child. Are you?" came her reply.

I had no understanding of death. Or did I?

Something was stirring up in my seven and a half-year-old mind. A woman was screaming and holding a baby in her arms.

"Who is that woman?" I said out loud.

"Woman?" said Sister Mary.

"Nothing," I said.

I thought best not to continue any conversation with her because I could see her gammy left eye looking in the opposite direction. This only seems to happen when she got angry. Normally it was quite happy, just squinting.

She gave me another little white pill and, in no time, I was beginning to like the effect that it gave me. I would fall into a dream-like sleep and be back in my beautiful gardens once more. I don't think they realised I was getting addicted to that little pill, because without it I was like some raving nutter, constantly throwing things at the nuns, screaming for my mummy twenty-four-seven and keeping the other children awake at night. But with the pill, I would be in a docile state, submissive, and sleeping most of the time, plus I was not too concerned with what was happening around me or what was being said.

In the magnificent gardens, the children I could see and speak to seemed very happy and comfortable in their surroundings. They ran around, like butterflies fluttering from one garden to another. This didn't seem to bother the adults who I perceived were supposed to be looking after them. Sister Bernadette, the majority of the time, sat under one of the trees that was overloaded with different kinds of fruit. As usual, I would run to her to give her a cuddle.

My arms would go right through her neck like it was the first time it happened, but I wasn't scared anymore. I could still feel her embrace, which I suppose may seem ridiculous to other people, but I know what I was seeing was real.

James was the first child to talk to me in the secret garden. He asked me if I could see a big bump on his head.

"No," I replied.

"Well, I have one before I came to this place, I'm sure," James said. "Em, it must have disappeared."

"Where are we?" I asked him.

He ignored my question and continued to tell me that he had fallen off his horse and broken his neck. He said he'd woken up and found himself in the beautiful place with the children.

"If I touch you, would my hand disappear into you like it did with my mummy?"

"Your hand will go through, it will not vanish."

He asked my name.

"Bridie."

"That's a nice name."

"I was called after my drunken father's donkey."

James laughed. His green eyes lit up like shining lights, like the ones in the orphanage grounds that were put on by one of the nuns once the darkness set in. His hair was shoulder-length, which I thought was quite funny for a boy to have. He looked more like a girl with it. James was still talking, but no sound was coming out of his mouth. Now his body seemed to be fading away from me into a white mist until it completely consumed him and all around him.

"Where are you going?" I called after him.

I woke up in my bed, pouring with sweat and still calling after James. My eyes were so glassy. For a moment, I thought I had gone blind. My head was pounding with pain as if I had been hit with something very hard, and I had pissed the bed again. I was so upset because I wanted to stay in the pretty place with James and all the other children, not to hear Sister Teresa with no legs' voice saying, "Sit up, it's time for a wash. You're smelly like the first day you came to us."

I ignored her comment and tried to get out of my bed, but felt like my legs were paralysed. *I bet that old witch did something to them when I was asleep to stop me from running away from her,* I thought to myself.

"How are you feeling today?" said Sister Cecilia as she walked into the room and plonked her big fat arse down on my bed. Her red face looked like she'd scrubbed it with a scrubbing brush. Sarah Moor, who was ten years old, said she was told once that Sister's face was that colour because she washes her face with the Holy Communion wine, or drinks it.

"I've been with my mummy and talked to James, and his bump is gone."

"Was you, now…?" she replied.

"The girl is deluded. She is the Devil himself," said Sister No Legs.

"No, I am not, and when I'm better, I am going to the new orphanage to live with them. You'll see!" I cried.

"Who's this James?" said Sister Cecilia.

Wow, someone believed me, I thought. I got so excited I couldn't stop rambling on. How James fell off a horse and broke his neck, and someone stuck it back on again. The fruit trees, the sea that had no waves, and didn't move, and of course, my mummy didn't have to wear the ugly metal thing on her neck and wasn't coughing up any blood because she must have coughed it all up, I told Sister Red Face.

"That child is pure evil, talking to the dead," she said, blessing her face with her crucifix about a hundred times, and shoving it in my face and telling me to kiss it.

I refused.

Sister No Legs got very angry with me because I wouldn't do what she asked of me and began slapping me around my head.

"Please, Sister, stop. The child is not talking to anyone. She is only having a bad reaction to sleeping pills. Best we keep her off them," said Sister Cecilia.

After four weeks in bed, it was decided by the doctors that I hadn't caught tuberculosis. I showed no signs of being ill or coughing up blood, so I was allowed up. Sister No Legs said it would have served me right if I had become ill with the disease because I knew I was forbidden from entering Sister Bernadette's rest-room, let alone sleep in the same bed as her.

Once out of bed, I went straight to my mummy's bedroom door and cried my heart out. I thought, *If only her door would open one more time for me, and I could hold her hand again.* I knew I could see her in the secret garden, but somehow it was not the same.

As time passed, my sadness got worse, and my behaviour was no better. I started wetting the bed again and didn't care when the other children called me 'piss the bed'. And to make matters worse, Sister Bernadette's name was never mentioned. The Bible and black gloves that she always left in the hallways had vanished, as well as the chair and cushion that she sat on at mealtimes. All gone. It was as if she never existed, only in my head and heart.

Looking back, I suppose I was grieving a mother who left me to rot in an orphanage and never wanted me, as Sister No Legs seemed to get great pleasure in reminding me. Not that I remember her, but every now and then in my mind's eye, I would see a woman screaming and crying with a child in her arms, while lots of fires seemed to be burning in a field. The pictures would disappear as quickly as they appeared. I was confused by them.

But I was lucky enough to have Sister Bernadette as my mother. She was everything a child could wish for in a mother, and I so loved her dearly, but I didn't have to be asleep to go into the special garden to see her anymore. I just closed my eyes, passed through the different colours like purple, red, green, dark blue, yellow, then white, then I'd be in the gardens. I don't know when and how this happened, it just did. It's like I could go into another world.

One day, out of the blue, Sister Rose and Sister No Legs told me to follow them. "Where are we going?" I asked them.

"To the graveyard where Sister Bernadette is."

I remember being very confused, but at the same time excited, thinking in my head that my mummy had come back from the secret gardens. I thought to myself, *Now Sister No Legs is in for it, for hitting me and calling me evil and other names.*

The three of us walked through a part of the grounds that I'd never visited and didn't even know existed. The morning sun was filtering through the great big chestnut trees. It was spring, and their sticky brown buds were just beginning to burst forth into green leaves that wound through a little black wrought iron gate.

The graveyard was very quiet. I'd never been in one before, so I didn't know what to expect. A great big wooden cross stood in the centre with a statue of the tattered body of Jesus hanging on it. Here and there around the graveyard were little alcoves with statues of Mary, Jesus' Mother, and a lot of other saints I didn't know.

"What are all the wooden crosses stuck in the ground for?" I asked.

Neither of the nuns answered. They carried on walking down a long path, and suddenly they stopped.

It had been several months since Sister Bernadette had passed into her new world, and now she had left it again, just for me. "Where's my mummy?" I asked.

Sister No Legs pointed to one of the little crosses and said, "She is laid to rest here."

I was getting more and more confused by the minute. Why would my wonderful mummy leave the beautiful gardens to be put under the dirty ground? What had she done wrong? She wasn't evil. Hadn't Sister No Legs said all bad people go to Hell, and wasn't Hell deep under the surface, and once you were there you are trapped forever? This is what the Catholic religion taught me, and now I was panicking. I needed to get my mummy from under the ground. I kneeled down beside the grave that had become overgrown with long grass. A cluster of wild daises were bobbing their heads in the breeze, plus a few yellow dandelions had opened their bright little faces to the morning sunshine.

The awful reality hit me hard. I couldn't believe my kind, gentle mother was under the cold earth. I ripped at the grass with my bare hands, trying to dig her up. Understanding was beginning to dawn on me. I suppose I knew that morning that I would never see my mother again. Well, not in this world anyway.

The folly was no longer my favourite place to retreat to from Sister No Legs' religion classes. Instead, the graveyard was. I felt safe there, knowing that my mother was buried there. The graveyard wasn't the gloomy place people would believe. I loved the stream that ran through it. I often paddled in the shallows, or just sat on the bank, dabbing my toes in the clear water. The water was so clean you could drink it, and I often did. When the sun shone on it, it sparkled as if the fairies had sprinkled their magic dust over it. I would spend hours trying to catch the little tadpoles that swam through my feet with my hands but never caught any. I'd watch the wild rabbits bobbing their heads up in the long grass as if they were spying on me. The woodlands that surrounded the graveyard were buzzing with wild animals. The ground seemed to be walking alive, carried by all different kinds of insects. I sat on a red ants' nest once and was bitten to death by them.

I found little tracks and paths that led out of the graveyard into the village. I had no desire to venture out of the convent grounds. The world that stared back at me was an alien place I feared. The nuns had told us that God had turned his back on the village people, because they were wicked sinners: with all their drinking and carryings-on, he was disappointed with them.

Nothing new here, I thought. *God seems to have fallen out with everyone, including me, so it was no wonder he has no friends.*

I didn't care what was going on in the outside world. They could kill one another as far as I was concerned. I was quite happy running barefoot through the woodlands in the home, picking bunches of purple willow herbs to put on my mother's and the other nuns' graves. I loved watching the little rabbits running to and fro around the wooden crosses, and sometimes I would see a fox who I called Fudge because of its colour. He or she had no fear of me or me of it. My life was here, behind the big walls, picking blackberries and crabapples, and trying to pass the time by blowing the dandelion clocks and watching the white globes of exploding seeds blowing away in the wind. This was my beautiful world now. Nothing to fear, only Sister Teresa with no legs.

First Holy Communion

The day came for me to make my first Holy Communion. I knew it was a very important occasion for me and all the other seven and eight-year-olds. We were becoming children of God, and would be old enough to know right from wrong, as if I didn't already know that.

I was dressed in a white satin dress with pretty lace socks, white leather shoes, a veil with beautiful white beads and a little prayer book. I wondered, once God had acknowledged me, would he bring my mummy back from the secret garden? Somehow I knew he wouldn't. It seemed quite strange that the convent walls were full of pictures of Jesus, Mary and all the other saints, but none of God himself.

I wished my mummy could have been there to explain about all the joyful feelings I was supposed to be feeling when I felt so empty inside. I was very worried about eating the body and drinking the blood of Jesus. After all, Katie William had told me that he had died two thousand years ago. I had missed so many of the religious classes; my imagination ran wild. There was no way I was going to eat a dead man's flesh. I had to create a situation where I didn't have to make my communion.

Angie Doyle said she didn't eat any kind of meat because it was forbidden in her family, so there was my excuse.

I told Sister Anna I wasn't allowed to eat meat anymore.

"Who told you that, Bridie?" she asked.

"God did," I lied.

"Well," she said, "It was a shame He didn't tell you last night when you were tucking into a big bowl of chicken stew and had the cheek to come back for seconds."

"But God didn't tell me until this morning. He was too busy last night doing other things."

"Oh, is that right? Did He also say you couldn't have cake and biscuits after the celebrations?" she said.

"No, Sister Anna. He said I could have double of everything, plus two raspberry lollipops, but not the body or the blood of Jesus," I replied.

"You know you must not eat any meat on Fridays and during Lent, and you know, Bridie, what happens if people do?"

"Go straight to Hell, Sister?" I said.

"Yes, that's right, and Friday is the day Jesus gave up his body so all mankind could live," said Sister Anna.

"Well," I cried, "That doesn't mean I've got to eat his smelly flesh, done it?"

"For God's sake, child. I don't know where you get your silly ideas from. Now come on, get in line with the other girls. Father Murphy is waiting in the church for us."

I stood next to Mary Doyle, who didn't seem fazed by the coming event of the day.

Come to think of it, nothing ever bothered her.

I decided that I was going to be strong and brave, just like her. If I had to chew a little bit of statue of Jesus, as Angie Doyle said, then so be it, and anyway, my second set of teeth had come through, looking like elephant tusks, and I was quite embarrassed by them. The older girls in the orphanage could be quite nasty at times, calling me names like 'buck teeth' and 'rabbit face' and many others. I pretended they didn't upset me, but they did. Sister Bernadette used to tell me I was the prettiest girl in the convent, and of course, I believed her. Why wouldn't I? But kind words wouldn't make my teeth any smaller, so maybe a little chew of one of the statues might just file them down for me.

I stood next to Sheila Carroll, who resembled an angel, all dressed in white, looking like God Himself had dropped her from the sky. She was drop-dead gorgeous with her red hair, pale skin, big green eyes, and dimple in her chin, but not as pretty as me as far as I was concerned.

It had been raining heavily the night before and large muddy puddles were dotted all over the ground, and the closer I got to the church, the more fearful I became. Seeing an opportunity to get out of all the pompousness, I jumped with a gleeful splash into one of them. Loud gasps came from the nuns, and giggles from the girls.

"You naughty, wicked child!" came cries from Sister Jane as she slapped me across the face and dragged me into the church to meet my Maker spattered in mud from head to toe. Grinning faces mocked me as I tiptoed with tears running down my stained, muddy face to make my first Holy Communion. They wouldn't be the last tears I would shed in the convent and, unbeknownst to me, there would be more in the years that lay ahead.

The body of Jesus turned out to be a piece of the wafer that looked like stale bread and tasted quite delicious. I wondered where Father Murphy put the leftovers. I thought it wouldn't be a hard task to get back into the church, as its doors were always open for the nuns to pop in and pray to their God.

The blood of Christ was cranberry juice, which was home-made by the nuns. All that tension and stress I had put upon myself came to nothing.

I knew some kind of punishment was on the horizon for me for missing all the religious classes. I was banned from venturing out on the grounds for a month, so that meant I couldn't go to the graveyard. I accepted my punishment for three days only, but when my chance came to escape the clutches of old Sister Rose, I ran like a mad March hare to my mummy's grave, only to be dragged back to the home by Sister Teresa with no legs, who seemed to be floating in mid-air even faster than usual. This went on for a few days until she gave up on me in the end. It may have seemed to some that it was a strange place for a seven-year-old child to want to be, but I was at my happiest there. My mother was there, and it was the only place I could feel her presence.

Family United

One cold Monday morning, I was going through the usual routine of washing, dressing, morning prayers, and eating the disgusting porridge for breakfast. Despite those familiar activities, there was a strange sense of excitement in the air. The nuns had big smiles on their faces, which was unusual. Normally they were miserable old dragons. Some of them kept kissing and hugging me. I thought maybe it was my birthday, but why were they cuddling me? I knew they couldn't stand me, and I swear they couldn't wait to see the back of me. I'd been in the home for five years, and not once did I see any of the nuns show any kind of affection or love to any of the girls. My mummy was the only one who took an interest in me and the other children, and we all loved her for that. She always had open arms for us.

Sister Joseph carried me to the Mother Superior's office as if I was a baby. She was a huge chunk of a nun, and strong as an ox. *Why is she carrying me? She knows I can walk. Maybe she thinks I have hurt myself*, I thought. *That's good, I can play on this and won't have to be with Sister No Legs for the day.*

"Oh, my legs are so sore. I think I probably need a bandage and a walking stick, like Sister Charlotte," I said, pretending to cry with pain.

"No time for your nonsense today. Best you listen to what I got to say, girl," said Mother Superior. "You were only being carried, so you don't do your running act. Now…" she continued to say, "… Sister Teresa is run off her feet with your constant roaming."

"I don't know why she keeps hovering around after me. She knows I will come in when I am ready to," I replied with a grin.

Mother Superior was standing very straight behind her desk with both hands hidden up the loose sleeves of her black habit. Her forehead looked smooth and shiny, framed under the starched white head-dress. Her round spectacles glittered brightly in the light of the tall sash windows.

A faint smile twitched at the corner of her small mouth. "Bridget, in a week you will be leaving us. I can't say I am sorry to see you go. Your father is coming all the way from England to fetch you. You are a very lucky girl. As you know, a lot of the girls here don't ever leave the convent." She said all that without taking a breath.

The enormity of the nun's statement took a while to sink in. I hadn't stepped outside the convent walls for the five and a half years I had been there. Now my father, the priest from the convent, was taking me to 'England'. Mother Superior continued talking, but I wasn't listening to her. My brain was running like a clock. Was England the little village I often stared out at behind the graveyard walls, where all the alien people lived? Why would the nuns want to send me out to them? Hadn't their God turned his back on me, as well as them? Would the aliens realise I was different from them? Question after question was pounding in my head. I could feel my heart beating so fast.

Mother Superior's screaming voice brought me back to reality. "What is up with you, girl?"

"I don't want to go out in the alien village with any of the fathers from here," I cried.

"You stupid child. It's not the priest from here. Your biological father is taking you to England, not the village. You will be going on a lovely boat for the night, and when you wake up, you been with your family once again. Isn't it wonderful?"

"Why are you sending me away? I only pissed my bed two times this week, and wasn't it me who retrieved Sister No Legs' slippers from the highest tree in the ground? I know she said they had been missing for over a year. Yes, they were caked with bird shit and falling apart, but I risked life and limb for her, just for her to like me."

"Well, you don't need to be doing your martyr bit anymore. Now stop your whingeing and go and get your lunch."

I ran as fast as I could to the graveyard. My eyes were blind with tears. I didn't want a new family; the nuns were my family, even at the times when they were physically and mentally abusive to me and the other girls, but we all accepted the beatings. We hated some of them but this was normal for us, and we all knew the older girls had it worse than we did. They worked long hours, scrubbing and polishing the convent floors, plus working in the laundry. Their days began at six in the morning and finished very late at night. They were treated like slaves. I often saw some of the girls going in and out of some of the buildings to do their chores. They looked dragged down and a lot older than their tender ages of fourteen to sixteen years. It was forbidden for the younger children to talk to any of them but, as far as I was concerned, rules were made to be broken. If not, why have them in the first place? I didn't see any harm in me saying hello to them.

Before long, I got to know some of them, and to me they were nice. I would steal handfuls of biscuits out of the convent kitchen for them. They nicknamed me 'the rebellion kid'. I didn't know what that meant, but it sounded better than the 'tinker's child' or 'tinker girl' which some of the nuns called me. But all said and done, this was my home, no matter how nasty they were to us, and of course, I was near to my dead mummy.

The day of my departure came too soon. It was snowing outside. I couldn't wait for breakfast to be over. Not that I was allowed any; I had wet my bed again, and the punishment for doing that was no breakfast and having your face rubbed in your pissy sheets. I wasn't bothered by the cruel treatment that morning. I just couldn't bear the thought of being taken away from my mummy and the wild animals like the rabbits and foxes that played freely around the graveyard. I just couldn't be separated from them.

I ran in sheer panic to the main doors – they were locked – then to the back ones. They were – also locked.

This was very unusual because the nuns would be going in and out of them all day long. I asked Sister No Legs why this was. She looked at me with pure joy as if to say that once I was gone, all her worries were over. Her explanation was simple – to keep me in.

"We don't have time this morning to play your silly hide and seek games. Now, go to the waiting room. Your father will be here soon to collect you."

I ran to the kitchen and hid myself in one of the big cupboards, believing I wouldn't be found. I had never prayed to their God, only my aunt Mary Helen's one, and didn't know they were the same God.

I was in such a state. I found myself saying, "Hello, God, I know you don't like me, do you? But please don't let them take me away from my mummy. I promise I will not steal or wet my bed again, or pull Ann Ward's hair out by her roots, or piss in anyone's bed again, and I'm very sorry for pissing in Sister No Legs' new slippers, and for telling Sister Marie she looked like the fat cow behind the convent walls. I will never, never be a sinner again, plus I will go to the religious classes to say hello to you every day."

My nine-year-old mind was running out of things to say to Him.

The cupboard door opened. I expected it to be God. Instead, it was Sister No Legs. "Come out at once…" she yelled, "you ridiculous child."

"I won't," I said back.

She called out for the other nuns to help her. Sister Elizabeth dragged one leg as Sister Ann the other and pulled me out.

"Sweet Jesus! What is the matter with you this morning? You can stop all this nonsense. Your daddy is waiting for you."

"I don't want to leave my mummy," I sobbed.

I was struggling and kicking at them. They both physically carried me to the main gate and more or less shoved me out of it and locked it really quickly so I couldn't get back in.

A very tall man, with raven black hair like mine, looked down at me. Sheer panic. I grabbed the convent gates and tried to climb over them, pleading to be given another chance, but to no avail. The doors were closed, the nuns had gone, and that was my life in the home finished.

He Lied

My beautiful secret world by the stream in the graveyard where my lovely mummy lay sleeping looked back at me from a distance, because of this stranger from the alien world.

I disliked him from the minute I set my eyes on him. He was trying his best to pacify me by saying what a pretty coat I was wearing, and if I would go with him, he promised he would return me to the orphanage the next day. He tried to hold my hand, and I pulled away from him. He swore to his God that he would gladly hand me back to the nuns. I didn't see any reason not to believe him.

Just then, a rickety red-coloured bus rattled and spluttered to a halt outside the convent gates. I had seen it many times when I stood peeping over the convent walls, but never dreamt one day I would go on one. The conductor took my father's money, rang the bell, and the engine roared into gear. I was so stressed I wet myself. As I ran up and down the stairs, the driver was laughing at me, as if he seemed to know this was my first journey on one. It was wonderful. Of course, my father disapproved of my bad behaviour, not that I cared. The expression on his thin face seemed to challenge me as if to say, *Sit down or else*. For a moment, our eyes met. My spirit rose up in defiance toward him. I decided to sit down, just in case he broke his promise to bring me back home.

The journey was soon over, and the bus swung into the docks and shuddered once again to a halt. I got so frightened. Aliens were everywhere; different coloured faces and sizes, and some were speaking funny languages I didn't understand. I presumed it must be alien talk. Some of them were sitting on big black suitcases, others buying tickets to England. My eyes were popping out of my head as I tried to take in what I was seeing.

A man with a brown weather-beaten face stood next to me in the waiting line for his boat tickets. His clothes looked home-made like mine. The woman he was with was very thin and looked full of anxiety as she carried a crying baby along in her arms. I watched her as she tried to tidy a loose strand of her hair away from her face, but the wind kept blowing it back into her eyes. She clasped hands with a small girl who was doing her best to pull away from her.

Four other children sat on an assortment of boxes and old bags around her feet. They all looked miserable and unhappy.

I wondered if their parents were taking them to some orphanage. Looking at them, a distant memory stirred in my mind of a family I thought I once had, but it soon disappeared around the shadowy corners of my mind. Question after question I asked as they bubbled within me. Who were all these alien people? Where were they all going? Was the world that big to hold them all? Was this the new world that God told the nuns he was building for the good people before he destroys the old earth?

"Stop asking me ridiculous questions," yelled the strange apparent father at me. "Look, people are looking at you as if you are demented in some way."

I didn't understand some of the words he was saying, so I left it at that.

I gasped in amazement at the big boat. It was beautiful. It carried many cars, lorries and humans. I never imagined something so large could float on water.

The family I had seen earlier with the half-a-dozen kids were standing out on the dock waving to an old woman on the harbour walls.

The very thin lady was crying and blowing her big red nose with a filthy-looking handkerchief that looked like it had never been washed. I turned away in disgust. The boat rolled from side to side. I expected all the pretty furniture to move, but to my amazement, it didn't budge.

Wow! I thought. *I can't wait to get back to the home and tell Sheila Carroll all about my adventure. She'll be so jealous of me.*

The sight of so much water overwhelmed me as I looked at the great swirling bluey-green waves. I wondered how deep the sea was. Did it go down and down forever? As the ship moved further out to sea, beautiful white waves of foam broke behind the ship like frothy lace petticoats. Seagulls were screaming as they dived for fish to eat. I remember my dead mummy telling me stories about the mermaids, who had lovely human faces, long, long hair, but tails of fish instead of legs. They sang beautiful love songs which, mixed with the howling wind and the roaming seas, lured helpless sailors to their watery graves.

I was feeling very sick, and my head was aching badly. I had had no food all day and nothing to drink. The stranger father got me a cheese and ham sandwich, which I savagely devoured. Wishing I hadn't, within seconds, I was puking it up all over my new shoes and on the deck. The smell of my sick was putrid. I couldn't stop heaving. I was tired, cold, and embarrassed. My brain was in turmoil. I cried to go home. The stranger father lost his temper and got so angry with me. He slapped me across the face so hard I fell to the deck. A middle-aged lady who had seen his actions looked at him with disapproval. She told him he should take me to our cabin.

"I don't fucking have one. She be sleeping on the deck," said the stranger father.

"Disgraceful," the lady said, wagging an accusing finger at him.

"Mind your own fucking business, you nosey old witch. Get your broomstick and fly your ugly old face away from me," the stranger father yelled at her.

Everyone was looking at us, and I'd never felt so ashamed about anything as the stranger father's bad behaviour. It was all my fault. *If I hadn't been sick, this wouldn't have happened,* I thought.

They continued to throw names at each other, until the stranger walked away, leaving me there on my own. I laid down near a corner of the deck. All my senses were under attack; my nose was disgusted by the smell of my sick, my feelings were assaulted by the cold rain, I was so tired I would have slept anywhere. The stranger father came back with a blanket and disappeared again. Try as I may, I couldn't get warm. It was getting dark and raining hard. A strong wind was blowing, making the boat rock furiously. I was feeling so sick but had nothing inside my stomach to vomit up.

I could hear the alien people laughing and singing. I felt frightened and so alone and wished the mermaids would come and rescue me. I was in two minds to say hello to God again, but decided not to bother. After all, he didn't stop the nuns sending me away in the first place, so would he comfort me now?

I didn't like the stranger father, but was upset that he had left me on my own and I didn't know if he was ever going to come back for me.

My eyes were feeling weary. I tried to keep them open but couldn't. I slipped into a merciful relief of sleep and was back in my secret garden. My mummy was there, her arms open wide for me to run into. I let myself sink into them.

"Get up," the voice ordered me.

I opened my eyes. It was the stranger father.

"Come on," he was now yelling, "Move your fucking arse!"

I looked at him with complete discontent and wondered whether all the alien people were rude and nasty like him, but thought it best to keep my thoughts to myself.

It was still raining, and I was soaked to my skin. My teeth wouldn't stop chattering. I don't think I'd ever felt so cold and miserable in all my life. The sweets that Sister Jane had given me were wet and soggy in my coat pocket. The colour of my new brown shoes had run into my once clean white socks, turning them a muddy-looking brown. I looked like a child that had been dragged through a hedge backwards.

Getting off the boat was another nightmare. People were pushing and shoving each other to get ashore. It reminded me of the story of Noah's Ark, where all the animals were rushing to get on the ark, only these were not animals although they acted like them.

I caught a glimpse of the man with the weather-beaten face and his family. He was carrying his little girl on his shoulders and lifting her high over the mad crush. I wondered if he and his family were going to the same place I was going to, not that I knew where that was. The next moment he had gone, lost in the crowd.

The train to Manchester had arrived. I was glad to sink down into the comfortable seat. The train wasn't as beautiful as the big ship, but at least I was out of the heavy rain and wind. I sat looking out of the window. We passed farms that had cows, and sheep grazing on the green pastures and red poppies danced in their thousands amongst the cornfields, swaying back and forth with the rhythm of the wind. Big oak trees displayed their large branches as if screaming for someone to climb them.

The train squealed to a halt into Manchester Station. People seemed to be running all over the shop, trying to catch trains from all different platforms. I was so scared I cried to stranger father to take me home. He grabbed my arm so tightly I thought he would break it.

"You be home soon, so shut that whingeing up, or you will get a fucking backhander."

I didn't know what he was talking about, but by the look on his face, it didn't sound too good, but I carried on crying anyway.

A young girl around eight or nine years old was sitting in a chair that had great big wheels. She had no legs. A woman was pushing her chair for her. I had never seen anything like it before and wondered where her legs were. I smiled at her. She waved her hand at me, then disappeared into another mad rushing crowd.

Outside Manchester Piccadilly Station, my tears soon stopped. I had to keep rubbing my eyes to get my vision in line. The sight I was seeing was just so beautiful; lights twinkling around buildings and over shops and restaurants, the colours were so pretty, just like rainbows dancing. They fluttered and flashed as though suspended in mid-air, a bit like Sister No Legs, who seemed to float instead of walk.

I was so entranced.

Is England a magic place where fairies and the little people lived? I thought. Big green trees were dotted here and there with lots of colourful balls hanging from them. Everything seemed to glitter and sparkle and glow. *Yes, I am in fairyland,* I told myself.

I couldn't wait to get back to the orphanage and tell Julia Matthews about my trip to where the fairies lived. She'd be so envious; she'd be begging to be my best friend. Julia was a year older than me. She had a big head like a turnip, and somehow her hair seemed to be stuck to it. Her big bulging eyes looked like they were going to pop out of their sockets at any moment, and she had the cheek to call me ugly, but she had a lot of friends in the home, and I needed friends. She was one big bully, and some of the children in the home were terrified of her. She made a girl eat ants one day, so to get her back for what she did to the girl, I dug up some worms and made her eat one. The rest I put in her bed. To hear her screaming was a delight to my ears and the other kids. After that instance, she never asked anyone to eat creepy-crawlies again. She believed that fairies came every night just to talk to her, and when she was living in Germany with her sick mother, she swore that she had seen a leprechaun in her mother's backyard. "What a load of rubbish," I told her, "they only live in Ireland," but maybe she had. I was so jealous thinking I had looked for one for years, but I wasn't going to tell her that.

Her best friend was Alice the Leg. She was called that because she had one leg longer than the other and had to wear special ankle boots on her left side.

"Taxi! Taxi!" Father said, as he put his hand out.

"What's a taxi?" I asked him.

"It's a fucking car."

I was thinking, *Should I ask him what's a car?* One pulled up and Father said get in.

I climbed in the back. Looking around it, I could see all the seats were black, and it had a black carpet all the way through the car. I couldn't help smelling the seat I was sitting on. It smelled of leather, just like the nuns' ones did.

I couldn't help noticing that the driver appeared to have a very large, white bandage wrapped around his head. Thinking he must have hurt himself, I asked does his head hurt very badly.

"No," came his reply, in a strange accent. "Why are you asking me this?"

Without answering his question, I ploughed in deeper. "Why is your skin black and ours is pink?"

The driver didn't seem fazed by any of my questions to him, and then I asked were all cars called fucking cars. I swear his face turned pale as he looked over his shoulder at me. I knew I must have said something wrong because the look Stranger Father gave me ran shivers down my body.

"My, my. Where did a little girl like you learn a very bad word like that?" said the driver.

"He keeps saying it." I pointed to my apparent father sitting in the passenger seat.

The driver said nothing; he just gave my father a disapproving look and carried on his conversation with me.

He asked what I was getting for Christmas.

"We don't receive gifts in the orphanage. The nuns said that was Jesus' day, but we did get an orange. I don't like oranges, so I gave mine to Karen O'Brian for one of her biscuits." I kept blabbering on, till Father told me to stop irritating the poor driver.

"She's fine. Every child should have a Christmas present," said the driver.

"Including me?" I asked.

"Of course."

"Can I have one for my mummy, too, please?" There's me thinking he's going to give me one there and then.

"What do you think your mother would like?" he asked.

"She likes bluebells."

"Wow! What pretty flowers."

I told the driver I always picked big bunches of them for her when she was poorly, but now that she was dead, I put them on her grave. "She didn't like daisies, so I've got to keep ripping them up from around her wooden cross."

"I'm sorry your mother has passed," said the taxi man, giving the man called Father a sympathetic look.

"She hasn't passed anywhere, she's dead," I piped up.

Father looked embarrassed. He explained that I had been away for quite some time, and my new mother and my siblings couldn't wait to see me.

The taxi pulled up outside an ugly red-brick house in a long Victorian terraced street. The house looked so small compared to the convent home.

Father bundled me through the front door of the house. I panicked and tried to run back out. He grabbed me by my earlobe and threatened he would kick the shit out of me if I ever tell a stranger or anyone else of my tales of woe again.

I didn't have a clue what he was talking about and was going to say so until I glanced up at his face. It was red with rage. His mouth was frothing, like the horses that live in the stables on the opposite field of the orphanage. The bags under his eyes changed colour as blue veins started to appear.

Still latching onto my earlobe, he pulled me into a room. "This is your mother's and my bedroom. You and the others aren't allowed in here, only on my say-so."

The living room only had two old armchairs and one very long table. There was a square of carpet in the centre of the room and around its perimeter, the floorboards were covered by offcuts offline. At the end of the room was a large black stove with a kettle on it. Above the stove hung a large cracked mirror.

I followed him to the kitchen. It was a complete dump; old, smelly clothes were scattered on the filthy floor, and the one piece of furniture, a chair which only had three legs, was propped up against the wall.

The water dripped from the single tap in a low stone sink. There was a small window, and next to it was a door, which led into the backyard. Another door led down into a cellar where the firewood and coal were kept.

I thought to myself, *Why is he showing me his dumpy house? I'm going home tomorrow.*

As we made our way back to the living room, my eyes beheld four half-dressed children standing at the table. There were no chairs for them to sit on. A girl a lot older than myself was spreading something on slices of bread. It looked disgusting, but I was so hungry because I hadn't eaten since the night before. My tummy was making peculiar noises.

"This is your sister Bridie," Father said.

Four pairs of eyes looked me over in silence; then they returned to their bread.

I wondered if I was going to be offered a slice. Another girl walked into the room. She was about fifteen years old and very pretty, with a mop of mousey-coloured hair and big blue eyes.

"Do you remember me, Bridie?" the girl asked. I shook my head.

"Well, I'm Libby, and that's Ocean feeding some of your brothers and sisters, and the one that just walked into the kitchen is Kelly."

My three older sisters were just beautiful-looking, making me feel quite plain and ugly.

"Don't you remember any of us?" said Ocean.

"Sorry, I don't."

I kept looking at the bread, seeing the slices disappearing fast down the children's bellies. I wasn't quite sure to ask for a slice or just take one. Before I could make up my mind, Father came back into the room and asked me to follow him back to his bedroom.

A woman was sitting on the big bed nursing a baby. The baby made a contented suckling noise. At the sound of me coughing, he stopped feeding, snatching himself off the woman's nipple to gaze at me with curiosity. A trickle of milk ran down his fat cheeks, and flame-jets of milk sprayed in several directions from the overflowing breast. I couldn't take my eyes off the woman's titties: they were so big. I wondered, *Would mine get like that?* I hoped not.

Although the woman was seated, I could see she was quite tall. Her hair was raven black and hung down to her big hips. Her eyes were startlingly blue, just like the fat baby's. She had strange markings on her long legs, like noughts and crosses.

"Do you recognise your mother?"

I was baffled for a moment, and thought who was he talking about?

"My mummy is dead," I replied.

"This is your fucking mother, not the nun in the poxy home," he screamed at me.

"Have you got any recollection of me?" asked the woman.

The strange thing was I did. Seeing her there with a baby in her arms brought memories flooding back into my mind. Wagons, muddy fields, children dancing, all mixed up in my head like a jigsaw puzzle. I couldn't acknowledge I knew this woman. I felt I would be disrespecting the only mother I'd known, who had cared for me, who was always there when I was poorly, who had cradled me in her arms when I got drunk on the Holy Communion wine in the orphanage. She was my life. I told the woman no.

The woman scowled briefly at me and turned the fat baby around to feed on her other nipple. His eyes rolled up in his head in sleepy contentment as his chubby hand pulled at the buttons on the woman's blouse. He soon lost interest in me and fell blissfully asleep.

In the corner of the room stood a black box. Father touched a knob on it, and all of a sudden, there was what I believed to be the little people running after a ball. I screamed with excitement.

All those years in Ireland, I'd never seen one. *No wonder, they had been hiding in this box,* I thought.

I ran to the box and tried to open the back to get them out. There were loads of them – 'Leprechauns'.

"Are you for fucking real?"

"Leave her be, John Paul. This is all new to her. In time she'll understand," said the woman. "Libby!" she called out. "Get your sister to bed; she looks tired."

I followed Libby up the stairs and into the room they called 'girls only room'. It stank of urine. In the centre was the most enormous bed I had ever seen. Four of us would be sharing it: Ocean, Kelly, Nancy, and me. Libby had a single one for herself. Two big cupboards stood in each of the corners, not that any of them had a lot of garments in them. The floor was uncarpeted, just grubby floorboards. The room was lit by a dim light bulb dangling from a long flex in the centre of the dirty ceiling. There was no heating in any of the rooms. The only fire was in the front room. The house was freezing.

Libby was the eldest of all the girls. Her pearly-white teeth seemed to dazzle you every time she spoke. God, how I wished I looked like her.

Ocean was the second eldest. She was around fourteen years with mousey-coloured hair that seemed to suit her pale complexion. She had a nice smile and walked with a limp due to rickets in her left leg. Since childhood, she'd worn metal callipers on her leg. It didn't seem to bother her.

Kelly was very shy and spoke to me with a soft, childlike voice. She was tall and a mirror image of Libby.

Nancy was five years old and a real little cutie. Her blue eyes looked sad and miserable. She had hair that was as white as snow. She was a child of few words. For the first six months I was with them, she never spoke a word or expressed any kind of emotion. I remember once opening her mouth to see if she had a tongue.

Considering we were all sisters, I didn't resemble any of them. I was the odd one out, in looks anyway.

My eyes began to feel heavy. I laid down on the bed with all my clothes on. Ocean put a load of old coats over me, and I fell into an exhausted sleep.

The next morning I dived out of bed and ran down the stairs. I was very excited at the thought of going back to Ireland.

The Ugly House

Father was in the kitchen, puking up in the sink. I told him I'd had a great time with his family, but I would like to go home now. Please can we go soon, I asked.

"Are you for fucking real?" he yelled at me.

"You shouldn't use them bad word like the taxi man said. It's very rude," I said boldly.

He drew his hand and punched me so hard on the side of my head my ears rang. I was a bit woozy for a few seconds and felt something warm running down my neck. Blood was pouring out of my right ear.

"I hate you!" I screamed at him. "You promised!" I cried.

"Well, I lied," he said.

He grabbed me by the throat, trying to choke me. I couldn't breathe. I could feel my little body going all limp; then, he let go. I laid on the floor in a heap, completely shocked and terrified of this man.

"Get up!" he yelled. "Go and help your sisters with the other kids."

I struggled to my feet. The pain in my head and ear was unbearable. Kelly shoved a piece of old rag into my ear to stop the bleeding. After a few hours, it did the trick. There were no painkillers in the house to ease the thumping headache. I laid back down on the bed and fell asleep.

I was so miserable as the days and months passed. I disliked Father and New Mother with a passion. They were never there for their children. The local pubs seemed to be their first priority. Not that they had money to waste on drink. Father wasn't working due to some back problem, he never had. He was receiving Welfare money to pay the bills and feed his family. He'd done none of that. The house was overcrowded with children. New Mother had no interest whatsoever in her family and her home.

We lived in squalor. My older sisters did their best to keep it tidy, but with twelve children, it was almost impossible.

New Mother was pregnant again. I wondered where it was going to sleep. The house was only a four-bedroom house, and we were all cramped in it as it was, let alone bringing another poor kid into it.

My sisters and I would get up as soon as the sun rose. We'd creep downstairs, praying we wouldn't wake our parents up, especially if they had bad hangovers from their night's drinking. All hell would break, and we knew one of us was going to get a beating, so we did our best to get on with the household chores without making any noise.

My job was to clean out and light the range fire. It was the life and soul of the family and the only source of hot water for what would soon become a constant demand for babies' bottles throughout the day. The little ones were lucky; they lived on the free powdered milk that the Welfare gave to my parents. The rest of us went hungry until New Mother or Father got out of bed and unlocked the big cupboard where the food was kept, and then you were given very little. Many times myself and my two younger brothers, Martinlee and Keith, would walk the streets looking for bits of food that some people would throw out for the birds. The food that we found we would eat very slowly and pretend it was something delicious, but in reality, it would be old apple cores, rotting banana peels, or bits of stale bread that hurt our throats as we tried to swallow it. It was no wonder we always had sick tummies, but when you are starving, you eat anything to survive, and the three of us did.

We thought life wouldn't get any worse than this, but how wrong we were.

Father decided that Martinlee, Keith, and I should help to keep the house and our siblings provided with food and money. Every morning he would kick us out the front door with orders as to which food to steal for New Mother and him.

"Sausages, eggs, bacon, all that palaver. For the rest, get any shit, and don't forget a bottle of sterilised milk. Any money ye get for begging, don't fucking spend a penny of it. If I find out ye did, a good hiding is waiting for ye. Now fuck off," he said.

My first episode of stealing out of shops didn't go well. I had stolen six eggs, taken them out of the box, and put them in my coat pocket and run out of the store. On reaching the street, I fell over, and of course, the eggs broke in my pocket. The yolks were dripping down my legs. I was devastated, not because I'd cut my knee, but at the thought of going back with nothing. My brother Martinlee came to my rescue.

"Look," he said, "stop crying. I got them, but next time keep them in the box, okay?"

Martinlee was seven years old. He was wild and reckless and rebellious. He had no fear of anyone other than his mother, who, for some unknown reason, hated him. He couldn't look at her without her going crazy and beating into him. He'd try to avoid her like the plague. He only had to hear her voice and would tremble with fear. I could never understand why she was like that to him in particular. He was such a gentle soul to his younger siblings. The fruit that he stole, he would hide away, and when our parents and elder sisters were not around, he would share it with the young ones. He suffered from curvature of the spine and was always in pain. On very cold days, his back would be bent over with discomfort, which made it difficult for him to walk at times, but like a little true trooper, he carried on regardless. Well, he had no choice.

Brother Keith was small for his six years, but that didn't stop him telling his father or mother come to that, what he thought about them. He would call them "fecking monsters" to their faces. However many times he was beaten, he still came back at them, only to be hit again. As far as Keith was concerned, he was someone special, and when he got older, he was going to gouge Father's eyes out and play marbles with them. How his thin, small body endured all the beatings and punches, only God knows. Maybe he *was* someone special.

My brothers became my best friends. We were always together. They taught me how to steal and beg, and in the end, I became a streetwise kid like them.

Day after day, we came home with our pockets bulging with provisions to feed the family. I didn't mind being sent out to commit crime anymore. It got me away from the depressing madhouse and the violence that came with it.

We came home one night, and the ambulance was outside our door once again. One of the front windows was smashed. The ambulance man brought Mother out in a stretcher. They were concerned she was losing her baby. Of course, my parents were drunk and had got into one of their nasty fights. Her eye was black, and Father's face was full of scratches. I had no emotional feelings at what I saw. It was an everyday occurrence with them. They didn't consider how their drunk behaviour was affecting their children. The little ones would scream and sob their little heads off for hours. My three elder sisters would make themselves busy cleaning up the smashed beer bottles and trying to get some kind of order in the madhouse again.

Martinlee and Keith and I would lay sleeplessly on the girls' bed, staring at the cracked ceiling, listening to our parents rowing. We would talk about if we survived the beatings from our parents what we would like to do when we grew up. It was the only way we could keep sanity within ourselves.

Keith was going to be someone very famous, make loads of money, and have quite a few wives and a few children.

Martinlee was going to seek out a good doctor to make his back better.

As for me, I was going back to Ireland to look after my mummy's grave forever. We had so many laughs on that pissy mattress.

I Started School

My life changed a bit once I started school. There were two schools right next to each other, both called St Vincent's – one for the boys, the other for girls – and both run by nuns. I didn't like it there, but it was an escape from the madhouse and crying babies.

I couldn't read or write and didn't have a clue what six and six was. The nuns said I was backward and put me down two grades. The seven-year-olds thought it was quite amusing to have a nine-year-old in their class. It didn't do my confidence much good, but I was determined to learn no matter what was said about me.

All the children were well-dressed. I looked like a tramp that had been dragged behind a hedge backwards. I did my best to look smart but to no avail. Every night I would wash the only pair of knickers and socks I had to my name. At least I had something clean on, I would tell myself I may not have looked clean outside, but my underwear was. My other underwear that I came out of the convent with, Martinlee and Keith had claimed for underpants. We had decided sometime back that we would share everything we had with each other. One for all, that kind of thing. Mother got me a blue dress, even though the school uniform was grey. It came down to my ankles. She got it from some rag-bags from the Salvation Army. I looked a right div wearing it. Plus, she got me a purple jumper that must have belonged to a monkey, the arms were so long. I could see why the other kids took the mickey out of me.

Every time my dress ripped, which was quite often because I was always in fights at school, I would cut up old shirts that were used for the babies' arses as nappies, and sew them over the tears. It ended up like a multi-coloured dress. I thought it looked quite pretty. The nuns at school said it was an eyesore. I carried on wearing it because I had nothing else to wear.

Of course, I wasn't very popular and had no friends. The girls were frightened I would give them some awful disease. It didn't bother me because my brothers would say, "Don't take any notice." I was pleased their school was next door to mine. At break-times, I was able to talk to them through the fence that separated the schools.

We hated school because of the bullying towards us that we endured. Once we'd had our dinner and our little bottles of milk, we'd be out the gates like long dogs, as if the Devil himself was after us.

The streets of Manchester were more fun for us. The people didn't criticise the way we looked or give a shit how many lice were crawling through our hair. Some folks were even nice to us and gave us money to fuck off.

Other times, when we skipped school, we'd be in and out of shops stealing anything we would get our grubby little hands on. We'd become quite experienced and full of confidence nicking. It was like having a wash. As easy as that. Not that we washed very often. Once a fortnight, if we were lucky, Father would drag the old tin bath from the backyard. The five youngest would be washed first, and the rest would follow in stages. By the time it came to my turn, the water would be filthy and freezing. It was more like a dip in and out for me. We never had any soap – that luxury was for our parents only, which they kept under lock and key hidden away in their bedroom.

The nuns at our schools didn't seem to be bothered that the dirty gypsies were absent from their classes in the afternoon. No SOS was put out to the school's inspectors to say we were hardly there. The nuns knew quite well we were always picked on, but never seemed to punish the bullies. I hated the name 'stinking pikeys' that the older children called us. I didn't know what it meant but knew it was something bad.

Brother Martinlee thought the kids believed we were bad pirates. He was handsome enough to be one – a bit like Errol Flynn, whose poster he had stuck up on his bedroom wall, but better looking than him.

My teacher, Miss Richardson, was the Devil's daughter – a rotten bully that made my life at school a misery. She was a middle-aged spinster with crimped grey hair and wore gold-rimmed spectacles at the end of her long nose. If I was standing near her, she would say, "Please, Bridget, don't get too close to me, child. I don't want one's vermin jumping on me." Plus I always had to put my hand over my mouth every time I spoke to her. She complained my breath stank. The old witch was very fearful of catching germs, hence why she always wore white cotton gloves.

When it was her forty-eighth birthday, the children in our class brought her in little gifts, all wrapped up with pretty paper. Mine was in an old newspaper that Keith had pissed on and left to dry.

I had found four large worms under an old plant pot in our backyard. I'd wrapped them up very carefully and put lots of my brother Jeremy's old Sellotape around the paper to keep it all together. I handed her the present with a smile.

"Thank you," she said with a faint smile and a surprised look in her eyes.

73

The next morning at school, she called me a nasty child. I had to stand in the corner of class for a week as punishment. Can't say I was upset over it. My only regret was that I wasn't there when she opened my present. At the end of the half-term, she left the school to move to the Lake District. I was glad to see the back of the old battle-axe.

A new teacher took over our class, Mrs Daily. She was nice and very down-to-earth. She was in her early thirties and wore her auburn-coloured hair in plaits or sometimes braids.

Her face was full of freckles. I loved the bright-coloured dresses and cardigans she wore. She'd bring in all kinds of seeds and get us kids to put them in jam jars with blotting paper and a little water and wait for them to grow. I really enjoyed waiting for my seeds to grow and bear fruit. It filled me with wonder.

Once a week, she had what she called a nature table. It displayed fascinating treasures brought in by eager-to-please pupils. Each exhibit was carefully labelled by Elizabeth Bagg, who had the neatest handwriting in the class.

Among the cherished articles were a house martin's egg, tadpoles, a red admiral, butterfly moss and Brian Robson's prized shark skin.

Sometimes Mrs Daily would take us on a nature walk to a park down the road from the school, and the children would return with bunches of weeds, grass, buttercups and caterpillars. Having examined the specimens, the children would be asked to draw pictures of them and make an interesting display to pin on the classroom walls.

I loved drawing. It was the only thing I was good at and which occasionally earned me a word of praise or admiration from Mrs Daily. How good I felt to be praised and to see my drawing pinned on the walls.

I began to love going to school.

In the winter months, the class was heated by a black stove like my family had in our home. It would crackle and hiss and spit and give off a lovely heat if you happened to be lucky enough to be sitting right next to it, which I made sure I was. If it had been snowing outside, there would be rows of wet gloves steaming dry on the fireguard after the snowball fight in the playground. The stove was the centre of warmth and comfort to me in my bleak school days. It took the place of my mother's comfort, and the cheery glow was as vital to the classroom as the heartbeat is to the body.

One day the school had run out of coal, and all the children were sent home. I collected brothers Martinlee and Keith from their school next door.

It was a complete shock to find Mother home. Brother Martinlee said the pub must have run out of beer. Mother was cold sober. I thought she'd probably had another one of her breakdowns. Whatever was up with her, she was home and had the stove burning brightly. On top of it was a pot of delicious lumpy porridge for us. All the younger children were gathered around the open stove watching the flames roar up the flue, holding jars of lukewarm tea thawing their cold hands. This was the nearest thing to happiness that I felt in the ugly house, but all good things sometimes come to an end.

Within a few days, she got bored with her whingeing kids. I assumed the pubs must have got beer in them again. Father hadn't been around for some days, and all she was worrying about was that he was flirting with other women, which he was well-known to do. Mother had it in her head that he was looking for a new wife. I could never understand why she loved Father so much when he was very bad to her and the children.

She was a very insecure person and was not very comfortable in her own skin. She would belittle her daughters just to make herself feel better about her looks, calling them ugly-faced bastards and telling us that no man in his right mind would look at us twice. I couldn't help wondering whether she was a bit jealous of them.

Mrs Daily was only a temporary teacher. Once the new term had started, she had left. I didn't return to school after that, there was no point.

There was an old semi-detached house a few miles from the school. It had been empty for years and had fallen into disrepair. The lower windows had long been smashed out by bored children in the neighbourhood. The council had boarded them up and put a big sign saying 'Keep out'.

At the back of the property, some of the wood had come off. Brother Martinlee and myself climbed in. It had become our beautiful palace, our sacred hideout, our shelter from life's storms, our fortress, a place to bask in the sweetness of our solitude, away from bullying, from school and beatings from our parents, plus the rows and screaming kids.

Downstairs was very dark and smelly and damp. Up the stairs, the sun shone through the roof, and the windows were open to the sky, but we didn't care about any of this. I was a princess in my palace. I found a couple of wooden boxes that became the table and chairs, and an old flea-ridden mattress was our bed. We pinched handfuls of flowers from people's gardens and put them in a tin that Brother Keith found in the backyard. We stole a large carpet that was up for sale outside a second-hand shop. How we got away with that only God knows. We nicked sheets and blankets from people's lines.

Within no time, our secret room was complete. How wonderful it was for us to escape from reality for a few hours each day.

Screaming Babies

When our parents were drunk, the violent arguments and issues brought forth from the previous night would scare the shit out of us. The babies screaming, windows smashing, older sisters trying to comfort the little ones. Of course, some neighbours would call the police and Father would be taken away in a Black Maria, Mother still calling him all the fuck-faces under the sun. Our Nancy and I would be hiding under our bed whilst all this was going on. It became a recurrent event almost every night in the madhouse. There was no happiness or love for us, only beatings and hunger, hence why Brother Keith gave it the name 'House of Horror'.

One Wednesday afternoon, we were going home from a hard morning's begging. It was drizzling with rain, quite windy, and the streets were shiny and wet with puddles of water forming in the roads.

Ahead of us was a group of around twelve people stood in a huddle at the street corner. A tall man with grey hair and a white beard was carrying a sandwich board over his shoulders. I couldn't read what was written on it. I asked one of the women from the group. She read it for us: "Prepare to meet thy doom."

Another man was telling the soaking wet crowd: "Ask yourselves this question: What's wrong with your lives? I'll tell you," he cried. "You lot haven't got God. Without him, you die sinners."

A young woman was standing next to him, looking like a vampire had sucked every drop of blood out of her skinny body. Her face was so pale and her skin translucent that I could see all her veins showing through it. Brother Martinlee said she was a walking ghost.

Her long black hair was as flat as a pancake from the rain. Her voice sounded weak and tired. She spoke slowly. Now and then she would pause as if meditating and close her eyes.

"The world is going to end in four weeks' time. Nuclear bombs will destroy us all."

"What's a nuclear bomb?" Brother Martinlee asked me.

"The farts that come out of Keith's arse," I told him.

The woman continued to tell the crowd, which was getting larger by the minute, the signs that we all needed to look out for, like the ice in some countries melting, and global warming, wars, earthquakes.

"What's global warming?" asked Martinlee.

"I think it's an outfit that people keep warm in," I told him.

Brother Keith said, "Where are we supposed to get these global clothes from, and what do they look like?"

"We'll have a look around the shops tomorrow and ask them. Once they are pointed out to us, we can steal them," Brother Martinlee said.

The woman told us to go to church and ask our priest, he will tell us all.

"We will go this Sunday to Mass, and I am sure the priest will give them to us for nothing. He knows we are poor."

For a seven-year-old, Brother Martinlee was full of wisdom, I thought. He seemed to know everything.

"What if he asked us for money for them?" Keith replied.

"Then we will nick them."

"Do ya children know where you can get the food of life?" asked an old woman, who was wearing a green plastic mac with a matching rain hood that kept slipping down her beady eyes.

"No," I replied. "Please, if you know, could you tell us?"

"Hallelujah!" she cried. "Once ya tasted the food of life, you will never be hungry again."

"We are starving. Do you think we could have some of the food you were talking about?" Martinlee asked her.

"Of course you can. Follow me."

The three of us followed her, thinking she was going to take us to some restaurant or café. Our bellies were hurting with hunger, and we were so excited to have the food of life in us, we just couldn't wait to get the food down our throats.

Instead, we ended up in a shop doorway where the whole group circled around us and began praying.

"What's happening?" asked Keith.

"I think they're going to say grace first," Martinlee said.

"They are asking God to shine a light on us or something like that, but I don't see any of them with torches, do you?" I whispered.

"When are we going to eat?" Keith kept asking them.

Once they'd finished praying, the woman with the see-through skin continued preaching about 'fires and broomsticks' coming down from the sky.

"Jesus is coming in a cloud of glory!" yelled a man in the crowd.

"What happened to our grub you promised us?" Keith asked.

The pale-faced woman ignored us and wandered off, giving out flyers.

"We are here to do God's work. Jesus is coming! Believe me!" the sandwich board man cried.

"Well, he best come soon, I'm busting for a piss. Can't keep gritting my teeth… I'm in agony," said Martinlee.

We waited in the rain for ages. Jesus didn't show up, neither did the food of life, so we made our way back to the House of Horror, starving and soaked to the skin.

Monday Blues

Every Monday, it was my job to go to the baby clinic to pick up the tins of Ostermilk powder. Mother was given free special milk tokens from the Welfare people because Father wasn't working.

Steven, who was six months old now, didn't take to the bottle very well. He would struggle through his feeds sobbing, and spend the rest of the day throwing them back up. He was not happy with the sudden change of his routine. He missed the warm, milky snuggle-time with his mother. It was sad she didn't have time for him anymore. The pubs were her only priority. Mother was carrying again but lost the baby. Some days back, she was in the hospital for two days. Once she came home, she was sad and said she needed to go drinking to heal her pain. The rumours that Father was shagging a loose woman hurt her dearly.

I asked our Keith what shagging was. He believed it was to do with shearing sheep. "Where are the fucking sheep in Hulme?" asked Martinlee.

"Fuck knows, but whatever they are, I think Father must work with them," replied Keith.

Once we had all the four screaming babies in the big pram, we made our way to the clinic, which was a mile from where we lived. My sister Nancy would grab on my dress. She just hated having to walk so far and how the country people (non-Travellers) looked down on us as we crashed through the doors. My siblings would still be whingeing their heads off, which always set off the others. Sleeping babies in their posh prams and the prim mothers would snatch their little toddlers up protectively from the floor onto their knees at the arrival of the ragged, smelly gypsies.

Nancy often took books and toys that littered the floor. She'd quickly shove them down her knickers and in her coat pockets. She couldn't read, but had a fascination with books. She would hide her collection under the loose floorboards in the girls' bedroom. Every now and then, she would look at the pretty pictures in them, then replace them back in her secret place.

Mrs Dyer, who was in charge of the clinic, was in her sixties. With blush-tinted hair and very few teeth in her head, she really didn't like my family due to the fact that our parents were alcoholics. I didn't understand why it bothered her. She didn't have to live with them. We did.

I told Mrs Dyer once that she should go and see the man that my mother called the dentist. He would pull out her few rotten teeth she had left and give her ones like film stars. Well, that's what Mother said she should do.

Mrs Dyer wasn't amused by my advice and threw me out of the clinic by the scruff of my neck.

Today was no different. She still looked down on us as if we'd just crawled out from under a rock.

"Where's your mother?" she asked me abruptly.

"In the pub."

"And your father? I suppose he's with her."

"Actually, he's not. He out shagging sheep," I replied.

Mrs Dyer's face went all pale. She clung to her chest as if she was having a heart attack. One of her staff gave her a glass of water, whilst another was rubbing her hands, telling worried onlookers she was just having a dizzy spell.

She pointed her bony finger at me. "Get that wicked girl and her bunch of misfits out of my clinic at once!" she yelled.

We were escorted to the door with the babies' milk and told never to come back again.

I knew we stank a bit, but she had no other reason to be so horrible to us.

That wasn't the only clinic that showed us the door. My mother had to send us all to Alexander Road, which was near Moss Side to have our scabies treated. We were covered from head to toe with them.

The nurses would tell us to strip, give us a nice bath, and scrub our skin so hard we would be screaming in pain. Then they would paint our bodies with disgusting smelly stuff.

Brother Keith was a filthy fucker. He just loved being painted by the nurses, especially between his legs. He always complained his winkle was still itchy, so the poor nurse would continue painting it a bit longer. He had no shame as he stood there naked as the day he was born, with a broad smile on his face and his willy as stiff as a poker.

Brother Martinlee was quite shy and wouldn't let anyone paint his Willy Wonka. He would do that himself. The nurse would get embarrassed by Keith's stiffy and decided the next time we came that she would have a new nurse to help Keith with the stiffening problem. Keith couldn't wait to go back to the clinic.

A few months later, we were back at the clinic. We met Keith's new nurse. Her name was Sophia, but Keith nicknamed her Ten-Ton-Tess. She was gigantic in size. He was terrified that she might fall on him as she was painting him and squash him to death, but she cured his stiffening problem.

He refused to go back to the clinic again, saying there was no way Ten-Ton-Tess was getting her hands on his balls again.

St Patrick's Day

It was St Patrick's Day, the best day of the year for all Irish people. We had to go to church – I had no idea why.

It was said that Patrick was a fifth-century Roman British Christian missionary and the Bishop in Ireland. He was known as the Apostle of Ireland and became the Patron Saint of the county, along with Saint Bridget, who I was called after, as well as Father's old donkey.

Father Murphy, who was drunk as usual, carried on talking about St Patrick for two whole hours. You would swear they were best friends or related to each other the way he went on.

I was starving with hunger and bored out of my head. My arse was aching from sitting so long on the hard pews.

Sister Winifred, Father Murphy's sidekick, was in complete awe of him. She looked at him with her crossed eyes as if he was God himself.

She didn't like me or my brothers. She never said this, but I could tell from the way she looked down on us with her snooty nose because our clothes were always dirty and ragged. She couldn't see us beyond our filthy clothes. If she did, she would have seen we were really nice kids. Blaggards, yes, but good children who would help anyone in need and had to do whatever we had to do to survive. She didn't have two alcoholic parents who sent their children out day and night, whatever the weather, to beg and steal food to feed the rest of our family. Some nights, they didn't even know if we were in the house, that's how important to them we were.

We had to bring home ten shillings every evening on Father's command. If we didn't, we'd get a good beating from him with his black studded belt. We ended up with stud marks over our bodies. He'd swear we were keeping back some of the money – which we were, to give it to our older sisters who were planning to run away from the madhouse but needed money to take us with them. We would never grass them up, so we took the beatings instead.

Maybe if Sister Winifred knew how hard life was for us, she would show some compassion, but I don't think God blessed her with any.

Once the service was over, my brothers and I made our way to the stalls. Brothers Martinlee and Keith disappeared from my side for a while. When I finally caught up with them, they both had wide smiles on their faces. I knew without a doubt that they'd been up to some mischief

"Okay," I said, "what have you done?"

"Nothing."

"I know you have. Tell me."

"Do you believe in miracles?" Martinlee asked me.

"No, I don't."

"Well, before the day is over, you will," laughed Keith.

"Please don't tell me you've nicked something holy. You know that's a mortal sin, don't you?" I told them.

"Who said so?" asked Keith.

"I think God did."

"What about all the other things that we have robbed?" asked Martinlee.

"They were all necessary for us to survive, and if God likes us, He will forgive us," I said.

"What if he doesn't?" Martinlee replied.

"Then we are fucked," Keith said.

The three of us made our way over to where Sister Joseph was. She was my brother's teacher in school. To say she didn't trust them would be an understatement.

"What can I do for you three?" she said, greeting us with her usual suspicious furrowed eyes.

"Sister Gertrude sent us over to ask, would you like a cup of tea?" Martinlee said.

"Did she now? Well, that's strange, considering she knows I never touch a drop of tea in my whole life," she said, raising her hairy eyebrows at us.

Sister Rosemary said we'd probably misheard Sister Gertrude with all the excitement of the fun going on, on this beautiful St Patrick's Day festival, and presumed the children didn't hear rightly.

"Yeah! That's right, Sister Rosemary. We are so chuffed to be at the festival, she must have said coffee."

"What the hell are you playing at? We haven't even seen Sister Gertrude," I insisted to Keith.

"Don't worry our kid, we have, she asked us to get her some biscuits. All will be revealed soon," he replied with a crafty wink.

"How much are your rock-hard cakes?" Keith asked.

"Two pennies, and keep your thieving hands in your pockets so I can see where they are," said Sister Joseph.

She put her own coffee down next to Keith, who popped two yellow pills into it. The pills belonged to Mother from her doctor who supplied them to her every month for her depression. They were supposed to make her happy but had the opposite effect on her. She was miserable from the minute she opened her eyes to the time she went to bed. When she was drunk, we didn't know if she was happy or sad, because she'd be in bed recovering from a hangover.

"You are dead when Mother realises that some of her pills are missing."

"I didn't take them, Peter did."

By now our older brother Peter had joined us. We were bad, but he was fearless. Peter didn't care about anything or anyone but himself, he was in love with himself. He would spend hours looking at his reflection in the cracked mirror in the front room, singing pretty blue eyes at himself. He was so vain it was sickening. Father said Mother must have had an affair with the tyre man who lived down our street because Peter had big fat lips just like him.

I didn't know who was worse, Peter or my elder brother Jeremy.

My brother Jeremy was madly in love with a girl called Alice, known in our neighbourhood as 'Slack Alice' for sleeping with the local boys. The gossip about her didn't deter him from trying to make her his girlfriend.

One night she happened to pass by our home. Jeremy was sitting on the doorstep, smoking a cigarette. He said hello to her and asked if she liked Elvis Presley.

"Do I look like a fucking Elvis fan to you?" she said. "I am a Beatles fan myself," she said.

"I was just wondering," stuttered Jeremy. "I am a fan of them as well."

"Lying git," said Brother Martinlee, who was hiding with me behind the front door listening to their conversation. We were killing ourselves laughing.

The next day, Jeremy came home from work with a basin haircut style like the Beatles. Father said he looked like "One of the idiots from the Marx Brothers." Jeremy became the greatest fan of the band, but Slack Alice still didn't fancy him, until he told her that he was earning one pound, ten shillings a week at the cotton factory in Oldham. On hearing that, she couldn't resist him. Every Friday night, she called at our home for him to take her to the local discotheque. She dyed her hair red and wore tons of makeup on her face to hide her spots. The dress she wore was so short you could see her blue knickers that matched her dress.

Their relationship was good for about five weeks until she met my brother Jeremy's best friend, Gavin. Gavin had the biggest ears I had ever seen on a human being, and of course, his wages were a lot higher than my brother's: two pounds ten shilling a week.

Poor Jeremy was heartbroken by the betrayal. He sulked like a seventeen-year-old div for days after she dumped him. He sold all his Beatles records, his suit, and winklepicker shoes to his not-so-best-friend Gavin.

He went back to his old routine of using his greasy Brylcreem to smooth back his hair and putting Sellotape on his top lip every night to get it to pout up like his favourite icon Elvis.

Heading in the direction of Sister Gertrude's stall, Brother Martinlee slipped two of the remaining tablets into her coffee.

"What kept you?" she asked us abruptly. "And where are the biscuits?"

"Wasn't given none," Keith replied.

Father Murphy was in his usual state – drunk as a lord – and was entertaining the crowd by singing 'Danny Boy'. His voice sounded like someone being strangled. Most of the people had their fingers in their ears to drown out the racket he was making. It was such a relief when he was half-dragged off the stage for the dancers to come on.

The music blared out of the gramophone; the children danced the hornpipe beautifully. The second dance was the jig. That's when the miracle happened.

Sister Joseph jumped on the stage as if she was possessed, her habit pitched high about her knees showing off her black long johns. The crowd was in fits of laughter. As her legs jigged backwards and forwards to the music, Sister Gertrude decided to get in on the act as well.

She threw her walking sticks down and began hopping about the stage as if she was doing an Indian rain dance. I was expecting it to pour down with rain at any moment.

"Sisters, sisters! Don't you have any shame?" cried drunken Father Murphy.

The people all got caught up in the great miracle of the day. Sister Gertrude didn't need her sticks to walk anymore, let alone dance. Some yelled "Hallelujah!" seeing her deformed bandy legs healed.

One woman said: "The old nun should be made a saint because God looked down on her suffering and bestowed a miracle upon her gammy legs."

"She should be canonised," said another.

"I just said that, you stupid fool," said the first woman to the other.

One slapped the other across the face. Both ended up on the ground ripping each other's hair out, saying, "Who the fuck are you calling stupid?"

Someone threw water over them to stop them from fighting.

The majority of the crowd were unaware of what was happening at the front of the stage until some children started throwing the hard rock cakes at each other and into the crowd. By the end of the day, people were going home with bloody noses. Both the nuns were still loping around the stage with bright red faces as if a demonic spirit had taken control of their bodies.

Drunken Father Murphy had given up on the task of trying to persuade them to stop showing themselves up. He had fallen asleep in his large deckchair and was snoring so loudly I was sure everyone in Manchester heard him.

My brothers and I made our way home, promising each other that if Mother asked us about her missing pills, we didn't know anything.

The next morning at Sunday Mass, the nuns apologised for their bizarre behaviour, and could only put it down to being touched by the Holy Spirit.

"Yeah, you're right there, Sisters… the old whisky has the same effect on me!" shouted Paddy Ward.

The congregation was in fits of laughter over his comment.

Brother Martinlee was given the highest and trusted privilege of going around the church with the collection money plate. Father Murphy believed he would make a very good altar boy with a bit of training from him and the nuns. He managed to steal ten shillings without being seen. He gave the money to our parents for food. Of course, it was spent on drink.

Father Murphy got suspicious because there was only a half-farthing and pennies on Martinlee's plate, compared to the other boys' collections, which had shillings and half-crowns on them.

Brother Martinlee was never given the honour again, and him being an altar boy was gone with the wind as well.

The Mullens

Across the street from our house was a house I called 'the lovely home'. It wasn't the building itself, which was quite pleasant, but the family who lived there.

Mrs Mullen and her two very attractive daughters, Nat and Lily, were kind and gentle folk. Their father was away at sea as he was a ship's captain. He could be gone for months on end, and I think the family missed him very much.

Their home had pretty curtains on the front windows, which were sparkling clean. Bright tubs of red geraniums decked the front doorsteps.

I loved that family with every breath in my body and often wished I could live with them, instead of the two alcoholics who I had to call Mother and Father and live in the shithole we called home.

Mrs Mullen would always invite me over to help her do her garden, not that the garden needed anything doing to it, it was always immaculate.

The minute I walked into her glamorous home I could smell the food. Her table would be laid with delicate cups and saucers with beautiful red roses on them. On large plates with the same pattern were mouth-watering sausage rolls, freshly made cakes and scones, all waiting for me to scoff them, which I did like a savage.

Nat and Lily taught me how to play draughts and Ludo, plus I was allowed to play with Floppy, the teddy bear that usually sat on an armchair in the front room. I had no idea who it belonged to. I was allowed to play with it for a few hours.

One Sunday afternoon, Mrs Mullen called me over and asked me to follow her upstairs. I thought her request was a bit wacky, considering she had never asked me up there before. I followed her anyway.

She unlocked the door to a small bedroom. Inside were two wardrobes, a bed, and a large rocking chair full of different-coloured teddy bears. In the corner, there was a big wooden chest. Inside the chest were the most beautiful dresses I had ever seen in my entire life. The majority of them were pink and white in colour, and all in my size. Mrs Mullen let me try them all on. I looked at myself in the big mirror that was hanging in the hallway, and if I may say so, I thought I looked gorgeous, in spite of the black patch covering my right eye, due to lazy eye correction, plus I swear my two front buck teeth were growing bigger every day. If New Mother didn't hurry up and take me to the man called the dentist soon, they will end up looking like elephant tusks, but apart from that, I looked good.

"Are these Amy's clothes?" I asked.

"Amy? How do you know about my daughter?"

I was too embarrassed to say, "I see dead people," and apart from that I didn't like it, not unless I was safe in my secret garden anyways.

"We've never mentioned her to you," said Mrs Mullen with tears running down her face.

Seeing her cry, I wished I had kept my mouth shut. I would never have had done or said anything to hurt or upset her and her girls. I felt I had and said I was sorry.

"No need to say sorry, Bridie. You did nothin' wrong," said Nat.

"Let's go out in the garden. It's a lovely summer's day. We could all do with a bit of fresh air," said Mrs Mullen, still wiping tears from her sad eyes.

Once outside, I felt at ease again. The hot air was heavy with the scent of honeysuckle, and the glass of lemonade that I was drinking was sending bubbles up my nose and making me sneeze and giggle.

"Amy loved dandelion & burdock and lemonade mixed together," said Lily. "Did you know that?"

"No," I replied.

"I just hope she's happy where she is," sighed Mrs Mullen.

I was wishing they would stop asking what Amy thought. I was a little bit jealous of her, if I'm honest. I could see her running around with a beautiful white dress and gangs of kids to play with; I was dressed worse than a tramp as usual, with a dosser for a father and a drunk for a mother. I so wanted a little bit of that love the Mullens had for Amy, plus some more of the delicious sausage rolls that kept eyeballing me on the table. Mrs Mullen said I could eat more than a horse, and she'd never seen a child put away so much food in her entire life. I thought, *Lucky for her she didn't invite my younger siblings over*. They would have eaten her out of house and home, and that included her mangy dog food as well.

I learnt from an early age, keep your mouth shut and your eyes open, and mine were well-peeled on the last slice of lemon cake. Once offered it, I devoured it like a savage. I've got to admit that I ended up with a stomach-ache, but it was worth it. One of my older sisters would tell us all to eat today, because tomorrow you'll be lucky to have a slice of mouldy bread. I took her advice on board but felt a bit guilty for not saving some of the food for my younger brothers and sisters. I told myself that they'd got the disgusting powdered milk to drink in their bottles, so I hadn't committed a sin of being greedy. The guilt soon faded away as I sucked on a banana-flavoured lollipop.

"What's your favourite colour, Bridie?" asked Nat.

"Blue, like the sky," I replied.

"Amy's was pink. We dressed her in that to go to Heaven," said Lily.

Well, someone must have robbed her pink stuff. It certainly wasn't me, I thought. I didn't have the heart to tell her Amy was now wearing white.

I could hear New Mother screaming my name. I was sure the whole neighbourhood could as well. "Bridie! Get your skinny arse over here now, and don't facking forget to get the pound off that old witch!"

Oh my God, I could have died with shame. I knew Mrs Mullen heard her, but she pretended she hadn't. I was dumbfounded. I gave her a cuddle and said I must go. As I got to her door, she called me back, saying: "Oh dear, I almost forgot, your monthly wages for your help."

Help? I thought. All I did was eat her delicious food and play with what I now knew were her dead daughter's toys. I took the money and went home.

A few weeks had passed by, and I had not seen Mrs Mullen about until she came knocking on our door. She handed me a dress that I had seen in her daughter's clothes chest. It was just so beautiful with peach and cream frills, peach roses dotted all over, and a big peach bow hanging at the back. It smelled like the fresh flowers that grew in her garden – so sweet.

"This is for you," she said. "I know my Amy would have wanted you to have it."

My God! I felt like I'd been to Heaven and back. I had never owned something so gorgeous. I thanked her for the gift and said that her Amy had no pain in her head because the big apple that grew inside it had gone.

Unbeknownst to me at that time, Mrs Mullen's daughter had had a rare tumour near her brain. She'd had lots of treatment, but didn't survive. She had passed away at the age of nine. The same age I was.

I found it quite daunting later in life when I found out through Amy's sister Nat that that's what Amy used to call her tumour – the apple.

As Mrs Mullen was walking back to her home, my father came around the corner from the Red Lion pub as drunk as a lord. He set his eyes on her as if he'd seen the Devil himself. He began shouting abuse: "Look who it is… Mrs Long Nose. The old cunt who keeps peeping out of her windows spying on folks. Best you keep your face out of people business, you old dyke!" he screamed.

The poor woman was mortified as he carried on his abuse until she closed her front door. I couldn't understand why he was so mean to her. She'd never looked down on my family like the other neighbours did and was very generous to my family. She cooked cakes and sometimes brought over a big pot of stew now and then for the children.

"Well thanks a lot, you've fucked that gift horse up. Now you have to get your fucking drunken arse and get some work," New Mother yelled at him.

Shoes from Elsie Tanner

Father complained his back was too bad to consider any kind of work. His solution was to send his kids out stealing food once again.

I wasn't bothered by this. At least I would be away for hours from the madhouse.

The first shop we headed for was the new shoe shop that had opened in Piccadilly High Street, Manchester.

I was spoilt for choice: so many pretty shoes. I decided on a pair of bright green ones that had small, thick heels to go with my beautiful peach dress. I wasn't colour co-ordinating them, I just fell in love with them at first sight, and they had to be mine.

The shoes pinched my feet, but I thought I might be able to loosen them if I walked around the shop. They were a bit painful, but I could put up with it, I told myself.

I was just about to step out of the store with my bright green shoes for all the world to see, when a store detective shouted: "Oy! Where do you think you are going with them?"

I started running and tripped over the doorstep. The man took my arm in a vice-like grip and led me back to the shelf where I had left my old shoes. He picked them up like they were a couple of dead rats.

"Now, get out of my shop, you little tramp."

Brother Keith yelled back at the detective. "Leave my sister alone, you bulldog. Have a look at this…" He pulled down his trousers and did a moony.

It wasn't long before we found another shoe shop. This one looked very promising, or so I thought. I chose a pretty pink pair without the heels this time, but once again, the store assistant screamed, "Stop, thief!" I stopped for a moment to see who she was yelling at, and realised it was me.

Two store detectives came running as if they were playing some rugby match. Seeing them, Brother Martinlee knew he had to create some kind of diversion for me to get out of the shop.

Within seconds, the attention was taken off me and onto him. Martinlee was lying on the floor of the shop, doing one of his pretend fits – spit dribbling from his mouth, his body jerking all over the place, his eyes rolling around his head – he was very convincing. I almost believed what I was seeing was real.

Someone shouted to call an ambulance. The store detective was telling everyone to stay calm as he would be fine as he ushered all the customers, including Keith and me, out of the store.

Once the ambulance arrived, Martinlee made a miraculous recovery and took off running. The store detectives clicked on that we were working as a team and gave chase after us. My brothers ran in a different direction to me. Both men came after me. I got as far as the Granada Television Studios in Quay Street and nearly knocked over a very pretty woman coming out of them as I fell at her feet.

"Oh my God!" she said. "Are you all right?" She reached down and helped me to my feet.

"Sorry, I just slipped," I told her.

I could see the men were in easy reach of me. I grabbed the pretty woman's hand and begged her not to let them near me.

"They have been following me. They are trying to kidnap me and murder me. Please, miss, tell them horrible men to get lost," I said, pretending to cry.

"By gum! It's our own Pat Phoenix! Can I have your autograph?" cried the store detective.

"Bloody autograph?" said the woman. "The only thing you'll get from me is my stiletto-heeled shoes on that bald head of yours," came her reply to them. "Why are you following this terrified little girl?"

I stood staring back at them with a big grin on my face. "She was stealing from our shop."

"Were you?" the lady asked me.

"No, I was only looking at the shoes. I took my own ones off to try on the new ones, but him with the bald head wouldn't give me my ones back," I said through sobs but no tears.

My two brothers came into view. Seeing that one of the store detectives had a hold of my arm, he yelled at him to let me go, if not he'd be sorry. Martinlee was standing on one leg like a flamingo bird, ready to lash out with his kung fu kicks. His arms were flying all over the place as if he was being attacked by bees and was trying to push them away from him.

"Come on, Keith, let's show these two bullies what we can do, brother."

Poor Keith said he was too knackered, and his foot was killing him. A few days previously, whilst we were hiding up from Father in our bomb-house, he stepped on a nail, and it had gone right up in the sole of his foot, causing him great pain. We'd gone to St Mary's Hospital in Oxford Road and hoped that they would make it better. They'd put a plaster over the wound and said he needed a diphtheria injection, but couldn't give him one without his parents being present. We knew that our parents wouldn't agree to go with him, so he had to suffer the pain.

Miss Phoenix persuaded the three of us to get in the taxi with her. She gave the store detectives her autograph, and they cleared off.

She took us into a very posh shoe shop just around the corner from the one we'd done a runner from. The manager nearly fainted with excitement. Customers ran towards her. One yelled: "Oh my God! It's Elsie Tanner off *Coronation Street*!"

"She must come here a lot," Brother Martinlee said. "Everyone seems to know her."

She bought us a pair of shoes and socks each, plus gave us a half-crown. She offered us a lift home, but we declined. We didn't want her to see the squalor we lived in, but I suppose it wasn't hard for her to guess. One look at our filthy clothes and dirty faces probably gave us away anyway.

We thanked the kind lady with the bright yellow dress on and made our way to the shop, this time to buy food, not steal it.

"We must buy her some nice flowers and take them to her house to show our appreciation, plus she might take pity on us again and buy us new clothes to go with our new shoes. We know she lives in Coronation Street, but don't know what number," I said.

"Once we find the street, we can ask one of the neighbours," Brother Martinlee replied.

It was still raining once we reached home.

"You cunts, what took you so fecking long? Where's the food? I am fecking starving," yelled Father.

He was so drunk and looked angry as sin. He stood up with his belt in his hand coming towards us, but his legs wouldn't hold him up, and he slumped to the floor, much to our relief.

One of my older sisters helped him to bed next to Mother, who was still nursing a bad hangover as usual.

"No wonder she keeps losing babies," Brother Peter groaned.

Once Father was out of the way, we could relax. Instead of having beans with dry bread as usual, we all decided we would have a feast with the food we'd bought from the shops – cheese, ham, red salmon in tins that not one of us actually liked, angel cake and biscuits, all swallowed down with the four bottles of stout that Mother would have for her breakfast each morning.

For the first time in a year, I had gone to bed without feeling hungry.

Kicking and Screaming

I woke with a bad feeling in my stomach. I put it down to all the food I had shoved down my throat the previous night. Both of my parents were up looking like the walking dead.

Father was scratching his arse and farting. The smell of him was disgusting. I had to put my eyes downcast to the floor because he was stark naked. It didn't seem to bother him, but I felt ashamed of him for walking around the home with his Willy Wonka hanging out.

I told Brother Martinlee what I had just witnessed.

"God will punish him for showing his mickey off, especially in front of his daughter."

By the afternoon, the madhouse was back to normal – screaming children, house looking like a pigsty and Father and Mother making their way out the door to get their pints for the day. It was always a relief to see the back of them, but a nightmare when they returned.

Libby told me to go back to bed. She said I wasn't looking too good. I was quite tired, and that awful sinking feeling in my stomach hadn't gone.

I fell into a restless sleep. Angry faces, and crushing voices whirled around in my dreams. Someone was forcing my legs apart. I opened my eyes. It was pitch black in the room. I could smell tobacco and stale beer.

"Father?" I cried. "I am sorry for eating all the food and drinking the stout."

The person didn't speak, just kept dragging my legs to the end of the bed. I kicked at whoever it was. Was he going to murder me? Father had threatened that one day he was going to kill us all off if we kept disobeying him. *Who else would want to hurt us?* I asked myself. I just knew it was Father. He had gone completely crazy and was trying to push something between my legs. I carried on kicking and screaming, hoping my older sisters would come to my rescue. After all, they had eaten some of the food as well. But they didn't come to help. *Oh no,* I presumed, *they must have sneaked out.* They did that sometimes when all the children were asleep.

The bedroom door opened. The light was put on, and my brother Martinlee ran at my father shouting, "Leave her alone!"

Father picked him up by his arse and hair and catapulted him out into the hallway. He landed on his bad back and let out a high-pitched scream.

Brother Keith threw his piss bottle at Father. He always kept one in his bedroom because he was terrified of the spiders in our outside toilet.

All I could hear was bump, bump, bump. That was Keith's body hitting each step as he rolled down the stairs. He had tripped over our Martinlee, trying to get away from Father.

All went quiet. For a moment, I felt safe hidden under my bed with my sister Nancy, who was trembling with fear.

Father came back into our bedroom and managed to drag me out. He tossed me on my stomach on the floor. He kept his knees on one of my legs. My other one he pushed up my back so hard, I thought it was going to snap in half. By now, I couldn't scream out because somehow he managed to shove something in my mouth that made me gag. I felt something cold on my private parts, then a ripping sensation. The pain was excruciating. He had no mercy for me as he entered my little body. The lights were still on, and my poor sister Nancy had to witness his evil.

Once his dirty deed was done, he left the room with me still on the floor.

Sister Nancy crawled out from under the bed to comfort me. She may have only been a child, but she had a lot of savvy. She got an old jumper from the cupboard and put it between my legs to stop the bleeding.

Brothers Martinlee and Keith came back into the room to help me to bed.

Martinlee decided it would be best if the four of us shared the same bed, so if Father came back to finish me off or attack my sister Nancy, we would have the strength to try and fight him off of us.

The four of us laid together cuddled up in a ball under the smelly coats that we used as bedding. We were terrified he would come back up the stairs and attack us again.

I didn't sleep. The pain in my body wouldn't let me. I closed my eyes, but my mind began to race really fast, and I couldn't stop it. It felt like everything in the bedroom was spinning around me. I managed to get out of the bed to throw up. I crawled over to the window and opened it. It was pouring down with rain, and the wind was so strong outside, I thought for a moment it would blow all the houses in our street away. I wondered where my new mother and elder sisters were. Had they abandoned us? I wouldn't have blamed them because Father was very cruel to them as well. I felt too weak to crawl back to the bed, so I decided to stay put, watching out the window for them.

I woke up the next morning, still in a heap on the floor, with my brothers and sister staring at me, thinking I was dead.

Martinlee had the weapon that destroyed my body in his hand – Father's favourite grey penknife, father had cut my little private parts, to preform his dirty deed. It was covered with my dried blood. Seeing the look of horror on my face, he dropped it.

"Oh my God, Bridie. Your face is so swollen," said Keith. "What has that fucking pig done to you?" Tears were rolling down his little face.

"I don't know, Keith," I replied in a whisper.

My eyes were almost closed, and I was having a job seeing out of them. The rest of my face was black and blue, but the pain between my legs was worse. The jumper Nancy had got to put between my legs to stop the bleeding had stuck to the wound on my minny. When I pulled it away, the bleeding started again. Brother Martinlee gave me one of his smelly shirts to put down my knickers to help stop the bleeding. I was in so much pain and wished someone could take the pain away.

Sister Nancy said that she had seen New Mother had some tablets under her bed. She could try and steal them; they would make me better.

Wasn't I the one who was supposed to be comforting her? Not the other way around.

"The four of ye, get your fucking arses down here now and see to the babies."

We all struggled to get downstairs. We looked like invalids. Martinlee was in a lot of pain with his right leg, two of his toes looked like they were fractured and his back was covered in bruises, but his only concern was for me and Nancy. He was worried that we would be attacked once we got downstairs.

Poor Keith's face looked like a panda bear. Both his eyes were jet black. It looked like someone had got black boot polish and drawn circles around his eyes. The whites of his eyes were replaced with the colour red. He was quite scary to look at. I wondered how our youngest siblings would react, seeing his bruised and battered face.

We wouldn't have dared to look in the only cracked mirror we had in the house, because our reflections would have given us nightmares.

"Get your fucking ugly face over here," Father yelled at me.

I couldn't move for fear. My eyes were fixed on a large bowl that was filled with water. Somehow I had it in my head he was going to drown me in it in front of the other children.

"Did you hear me?" he roared again.

I couldn't speak. I thought my body was on fire, it was that hot. I felt like I was going to faint. The sick kept coming up from my belly to my throat. I was doing my best to swallow it, but in the end, it came out like a fountain.

The freezing water he poured over my head turned a dirty red. For a moment, I thought he was putting colour in my hair like Mother did when she dyed her hair red to cover her grey roots.

The back door opened. New Mother and my sisters and some other woman, who I didn't recognise, walked in.

"Oh, Jesus, Mary! What happened to that child?" the stranger cried.

"She got a bit gobby, so I gave her a few slaps," Father replied.

Father seemed to recognise the woman, who had a look of horror on her attractive face.

"What the feck did you hit her with… a hammer? Look at her!" the woman continued. "She's smothered in dried blood."

The lady walked over to me, picked up one of Father's old shirts, and began drying my head with it.

I burst into tears. It was so long since I'd had a cuddle from anyone or been shown any compassion, but here was this person holding me so tightly in her arms, I thought I had gone to Heaven and back.

"Don't you remember me, Bridie?" she asked.

I was frightened to say I didn't, just in case she got upset with me and withdrew her warm embrace, so I said nothing.

"I'm Mary, your auntie."

I looked into her kind eyes, but my mind wasn't interested in trying to figure out who she was. Instead, it was screaming out with pain, *Please help me!*

Auntie Mary was my New Mother's sister. She and her husband Ryan and her two sons, Charlie and Dennis, who were ten and eleven years old, had come to visit us. Uncle Ryan was hoping that he could find some kind of work in England, so his family could have a better life as he felt there was no future for them overseas.

He was quite a tall man, and always dressed in black from head to toe. He was a man of very few words, hence why he was given the nickname 'the Quiet Man'.

Once back in my smelly bedroom, Aunt Mary continued to wash the rest of the dried blood from my aching body. Seeing the old shirt between my legs, she asked me had my women's troubles started (i.e., my periods).

I didn't have the foggiest idea what she was rabbiting on about and said No. She pulled the shirt away. Her screams alerted Mother and Father.

"Jesus, Betty! You best get a doctor are take this child to the hospital," Aunt Mary said to Mother.

"Why, what's up?"

She pulled my blood-stained dress down once Father entered the room. Mother lifted it up again. I could have died of shame; I felt so exposed.

"She needs stitches. It looks like some bastard has slit her little private parts into two bits."

"Who did that to you?" Mother screamed at me. "Fucking tell me!"

"Stop yelling at her. Can't you see the child is scared to death?"

"You can tell me, Bridie," said Aunt Mary.

I kept my head down and didn't say a word. And anyway, I didn't know the words for torture and rape back then.

Father told Aunt Mary that my brothers Martinlee, Keith and me were always rummaging in bombed houses and that probably some old dirty tramp had got hold of me.

"Is that what happened to you?" he asked.

I looked up and stared into his bloodshot eyes. For the first time in my life, I felt true hatred towards another human being.

I nodded my head in agreement with him, terrified to tell the truth.

"I think we should call the police," said Aunt Mary. "That bastard needs to be caught and locked up before he does this to another innocent child."

"We can't call them in," Mother cried. "The Welfare will be involved. They will take all my kids away from me."

"Do you want that on your fucking conscience?" Father said to Aunt Mary.

Aunty Mary began to cry as she continued rocking me back and forth. It reminded me of my mummy in the cold graveyard in Ireland. How I missed her warm embrace, her laughter, her smile, her voice. If only I could get back to her. Yes, I could see her in my mind's eye, but that wasn't enough for me anymore. I wanted to run barefoot through the graveyard, pick bunches of bluebells, eat the disgusting crab apples that always gave me a bellyache, look for the leprechauns, and wake up with Sister Teresa No Legs hovering over me, saying: "You are having one of your silly dreams again!" But I wasn't dreaming. I was wide awake, living a nightmare.

My parents and Auntie agreed. It was best to keep it within the family for the sake of all.

Auntie bought some antiseptic cream to ward off infections, which I used faithfully every day.

The incident that happened to me that night was never mentioned again, not even by my older sisters. I somehow thought I would have got some kind of comfort from them, but there was nothing. It was like they were frightened to speak to me about the incident. A cuddle from one of them may have assured me that all would be okay, but my family wasn't like a 'normal' family. Whatever normal is.

Three of a Kind

Considering we were all brothers and sisters and lived in the same madhouse, there were three separate groups.

There was Libby, Ocean, Kelly, Peter, and Jeremy – they seemed to stick together and really didn't have much conversation with their younger siblings.

Then there was Martinlee, Keith, and me – we were the providers for the whole family, stealing and begging to feed them. Even though the three eldest were working and paying their way, the money didn't go into the home; it went into the pubs instead.

Jill was two years old, Chris three, Steven six months and Nancy five.

The three youngsters' lives were very simple: eat, sleep, shit and cry for the attention of anyone, which for the majority of the time they got.

Nancy was different. She would talk you to death for hours on end. She was wise beyond her years and loveable. She loved books, any books that were filled with pretty pictures, not that she could read, but they were her treasured possessions. Once she had finished flicking through the pages, she would wrap them in one of her old dresses and place them lovingly under a loose floorboard in the girls' bedroom until the following day.

I was devastated when Auntie Mary Helen said she and her family were going back to Ireland. Her husband couldn't get any work, and their savings were being eaten up by everyday expenses. I'd grown very close to her in the short time she was in England. Every day she'd have Martinlee, Keith, Nancy, and myself to her tidy two-bedroomed flat to fill us up with toast and marmalade.

Uncle Ryan would sit at the head of the table, eating his two veg, potatoes boiled in their skins and chunks of meat that floated in gravy. I've got to be honest, the meat stank, but he seemed to enjoy eating it.

A few days before she was due to go back overseas, she asked me and Martinlee and Keith if we would be kind enough to do a bit of shopping for her. She wanted six tins of Uncle Ryan's favourite meat.

"What is it called?" asked Martinlee.

"I haven't got a clue," she replied. "They got no labels on them. Just tell the shopkeeper they're for me, okay?"

Mr Echo, who owned the shop, must have been about a hundred years old. He was as bald as a coot with not a tooth in his head. His cat was a spiteful animal – it would sit on the counter guarding the rows of half-crowns and sixpences that his master would stack up in piles behind a large sweetie jar. My hands were ripped to bits because of his mangy cat. I gave up trying to steal some of the money; Blackie, the mad cat, had outsmarted me. I wasn't going to give him the opportunity of sticking his claws into my hands again.

"Sorry your aunt is going back overseas. Nice lady. Bet ye are gonna miss her?"

"Yeah," we said.

"What is she going to do with her cat?"

"What cat? She don't have one," Martinlee said.

"She must have one, 'cos them tins you got in your hands are cat food. I sell them cheap 'cos the labels are removed 'cos they're out of date. Everyone who shops here knows that."

We laughed all the way back to Aunt Mary's flat.

Once inside, I told her that Mr Echo was enquiring about her cat. "What fecking cat? That fecking old man is not all there in the head." We giggled as we relayed what the old fellow had told us.

"Oh, Jesus, Mary and Joseph! I've been feeding my man on shitty cat food! It's a wonder I haven't killed him off! Promise ya won't tell him, or anybody else at that."

We promised her.

Once the evidence of Father's physical abuse had disappeared from our faces, he practically kicked myself and my brothers back onto the streets to steal.

After a month of being cooped up, it was a relief for the three of us to be breathing fresh air again. Well, if you could call it that. The smog that came out of the chimneys from the cotton mills had a foul smell, which hung loose in the air and often left your nostrils burning. It didn't seem to bother the people that lived in Manchester. I suppose over time, if you live with something long enough, you get used to the smell, like I did.

I fell in love with the place, with its smoking factory chimneys, the evening newspaper sellers calling out the local headlines, the cinemas, clubs, restaurants, traffic fumes, the warm waft of beer and smoke as you walked past the pub doors of the streets of Manchester, the smell of fish and chips and the pampered perfumed scent of the ladies emerging from the hairdressers, but nothing could beat the favourite smell of the big, juicy frankfurters and the lovely chunky, greasy onions, all hot and sizzling. They were irresistible on a very cold evening. The short, hairy Italian man who sold them had a kind heart. He always bribed us to come over to his stall every time he saw us.

"Have ye eaten today?" he would ask us in his broken English.

"No," I replied, "But the butcher gave us some bones this morning for our dog. We're gonna boil them up tomorrow, so we got something to eat."

"Didn't know ye had a dog," exclaimed the Italian hotdog man.

"We don't," Martinlee said.

The old fella grinned at us as if we were telling him porky pies. We weren't. Every Saturday morning, we would collect the bones from the butchers for our invisible dog. We'd take them back to our bombed house, put them in an old saucepan we had stolen from our house, cook them the next day and share them with any old tramps that happened to be in the yard with us. I must admit they tasted delicious.

The Italian always took pity on us and fed us up. Once we had filled our bellies with the food our hairy friend gave us, we said our goodbyes and made our way home with the ten shillings we had managed to beg. The wind was very cold and making me feel uncomfortable within myself. My body was trembling inside and outside as if an earthquake was going on within me. I didn't know if it was the fear of going back to the ugly house or the cold.

Keith suggested it was probably both.

Before Auntie Mary went back to Ireland, she took me to see an optician. I still couldn't see properly out of my right eye. The optician said I had bruising at the back of my eye and needed to rest it. He put a ridiculous pink patch over my eye this time. I'd gone from looking like a pirate with the black patch to looking like a right prat.

Next stop, the dentist. He took my four front roots out, leaving me gummy.

Aunt said I screamed like a cat without anaesthetic. "No matter. At least the fecker left some teeth in your head. New ones will grow back, so stop your whining, girl."

I was sorry when she and her family left Manchester. All the laughter stopped, and Father began drinking again. He had taken the pledge four months previously, swearing to God he wouldn't drink for six months. Old Drunk Father Murphy even gave him a pledge badge that Father had to wear every day to remind him not to break his promise to the big man above.

It was no wonder we were terrified of going home. With Aunty Mary, not there to protect us from Father, we knew it wouldn't be long before the beatings would start up again.

We continued walking in the pouring rain until we reached Miss Griffin's shop. The bells jingled as I opened the door. The old shop smelled of rotting cheese and damp.

"What are you little maggots doing out this late at night?"

"That's one thing about the old gorgie witch… she has a way with words," Martinlee said.

"Have you got any camomile lotion for our flea bites?" I asked her.

"Stand there till I fetch it from the back room," came her reply.

Once she was out of sight, my brothers grabbed loaves of bread and put them under their wet coats. I managed to get another small loaf and margarine.

As I was shoving them down my knickers, Mrs Walsh came in with her Alsatian dog. Of course she'd seen what I had done and called out, "Katie, Katie! The little beggars are stealin' from your shop!"

We ran out of the shop with the brown Alsatian dog following us.

It wasn't long before it caught up with me and had me pinned up against a wall. I thought it was going to eat me, not that there was a lot to eat. Martinlee threw it a slice of bread to get the dog's attention. It didn't work. It still kept growling and frothing from his mouth at me.

Keith got down on his knees and called the dog over to him. "Are you fucking stupid?! Get up," Martinlee said.

"Just watch and learn…" said Keith, waving a slice of bread in his hand. "Look, you two, my gypsy spell is working!"

The dog strolled over, sniffed the bread in Keith's hand, decided he didn't like the gift being offered to him, and bit Keith's hand instead. So much for his gypsy magic.

Keith had a small punch hole in his finger, nothing to make a big deal over, but he freaked out over it anyway, saying he'd got rabies.

We had to keep stopping on the way home to see if his eyes had popped out of his head like a frog, or if his skin had turned yellow, or whether a lump had appeared on his back. He believed this was what happened to anyone who got a deadly disease because his crazy friend James at his school had told him.

I told him he needs a cork shoved up his arse to stop him from farting. He stank like a polecat because of all the greasy onions that he had eaten. No wonder the dog lost interest in us and ran off in the opposite direction with his owner calling, "Ben, come to Mummy" – to no avail, Ben was off like a long dog.

We reached home with a smile on our faces. No beating tonight for us. We could sleep soundly in our beds without fear. We handed over the bread, margarine, and the half-crown to our crazy father. Mother had gone to bed early, complaining of a bellyache, much to my brothers' relief. For some unknown reason, she couldn't abide Keith or Martinlee. She only had to look at them, and she would go into a screaming fit and begin lashing out at them for no reason at all. My brothers had accepted her hatred of them and did their best to keep out of her way. Unfortunately, sometimes it was impossible as they lived in the same house as her, but try they did.

We were terrified of going home without food or money. Lady Luck wasn't always with us. We would take our punishment like little soldiers. We would endure the beatings that were waiting for us behind closed doors. We'd tell each other, "He don't scare me!" – puffing out our little chests, straining to get a muscle in our skinny little arms – but in reality we'd only have to see Father take his belt off to hit us with and we'd scream like banshees. He wouldn't stop until he drew blood from our bodies.

On one occasion, Father believed we were keeping back some of the begging money from him. Unbeknownst to him, we were giving some of it to our sister Libby. She was planning to run away from the ugly house with Ocean. She said they couldn't afford to take me and Martinlee or Keith until we helped to pay our way, so every so often, I would give her a half-crown, hoping by the time she was ready to go that there would be enough to take us. Of course, we never volunteered this information to our parents.

Father disappeared out of the backyard. He returned with the old tin bath, filled it up with cold water, and told my brothers and me to strip. We obeyed and stepped into the freezing cold water, shivering.

"You will stay there until ya tell me where ya have hidden any money or who have ya been given it to," he said as he left the room, turning the light off

We stood in pitch darkness for quite some time. Our feet had gone completely numb. Poor Martinlee's back was aching for standing too long. Keith told him to stop whining like a baby. At least Martinlee wasn't dying of rabies – like he was. Every muscle in my body was hurting. I just wanted to go to bed and wrap all the old, smelly coats around me to find warmth again.

The door opened, the light went on, and Father stood in front of us. "Well?" he said. "Which one of ya has been pinchin' the money?"

"None of us!" I said.

My brothers said nothing, just kept their eyes cast to the floor.

Father walked into the kitchen. We could hear the tap running. He came back with a tin bucket and poured the contents of it over each of our heads. The bitter cold water took our breath away. New Mother came in and told Father if we had been sneaking any money from our takings, we would have owned up by now. She told us to fuck off to bed. We gladly obeyed her and climbed the stairs to our rooms, feeling weak but proud of ourselves for not giving him any information.

Of course, we were expected to go out shoplifting and begging the next morning. Instead, we went straight to our bombed house. Martinlee wasn't too well. He still had pains in his back and chest. We made him a bed on the old mattress and let him rest up for the day, whilst Keith and I walked the mile into Piccadilly Centre.

It turned out to be a fruitful day. We had earned £3 one shilling begging. We couldn't believe our luck as we had never been given that much money before. It was a fantastic feeling to be able to walk into a shop and buy the food without having the hustle of steal it. We bought our hairy hotdog man some pretty flowers for being so kind to us, and some Anadin pills to make our Martinlee better.

Our parents were quite pleased with the goodies we brought home. Mother held her hand out for money, and I handed her a pound note.

She told us to take off our shoes, so she could check them.

She'll be lucky, I thought. With the size of the holes in them, we had a job to keep our feet in them, let alone money.

The new shoes Elsie Tanner (Pat Phoenix) had bought for us, we hid underneath the floorboards in my bedroom with Nancy's unread books. We promised Nancy that if she kept her mouth shut, we would get her a pair as well.

We never mentioned to our parents about meeting the nice lady. We were concerned they would find out that we'd been caught shoplifting. We hated to think what punishment Father would bestow upon us. Best to keep our tongue at the back of our teeth and say nothing.

"Fuck off to bed," Father said, still looking at us with suspicion in his eyes. He knew we were keeping money from him, but he couldn't prove it.

Grandma

Grandma came to stay for a few weeks. She arrived on a wet Monday morning with her white pet poodle called Bimbo. God, it must have been the ugliest looking dog on the planet. It must have lived out in the Wild West, and the Indians had scalped him of his fur.

Father wouldn't allow us to have a dog or cat, saying there were enough animals in the home without bringing another one in. He was talking about his children.

Bimbo was wearing a small pair of glasses that were tied with plastic from one end to the other to keep them on his head. He was the strangest raggedy dog I've ever seen.

Father asked her where did she get the fucking rat from.

She hit him with her handbag and replied: "He may be half-blind, but not fecking deaf! Mind what you say around him. He is very sensitive."

You would swear she was talking about a human being.

Grandma was small in height, in her early sixties, and quite attractive. She wore her silver hair in a very tidy bun high on top of her head. Her complexion was pale as if she had no blood in her skinny body. She would put dots of rouge on her face to give it some colour.

Every time she sat down or got up from a chair, she'd fart and blame poor scabby Bimbo.

"Oh, Bimbo!" she'd say, waving her hand in front of her nose.

The dog would just look up, as if to roll its eyes, and lay its weird head back down again. The smell from Grandma was toxic. Brother Martinlee said he thought something had died inside her, and her body was trying to discard it. She'd drink Guinness for breakfast, dinner and supper. It was no wonder she stank the house out, not that it didn't stink anyway.

Father had to go and buy toilet paper for her because she complained that she wouldn't be seen dead wiping her fecking arse with an old newspaper. What would God say if she happened to die with the evening news printed all over her arse?

She slept in with the girls, but demanded to have her belongings in Mother's wardrobes, saying our ones stank of piss.

105

I helped her hang her clothes up. I was shocked by the amount of clobber she had: six cardigans, three coats, all in black, six pairs of boots and shoes, lots of baggy knickers and one skirt.

I could hear mother saying to Father, it looked like "the old cunt will be fecking here forever" with the amount of stuff she'd come with.

The household changed from the day she came to stay. There were no more beatings, and Father couldn't sneak into his daughters' bedroom to interfere with them anymore, as it appeared I wasn't the only girl being sexually abused by the monster.

We felt very safe with her around and could sleep without fear or worrying who he was coming for next.

She lay between my sisters and myself, telling us stories about our Grandad Pat. He was so handsome, she would say, and all the young travelling girls hoped they would catch his eye. She said the first time she'd set her eyes on him at Dublin Market in Ireland, she knew she was going to marry him. His family were there selling horses, and she was begging and telling fortunes. She walked over to him like a brazen hussy and asked to tell his fortune. She described the girl he was going to marry – of course, she was describing herself.

They married two years later when she was sixteen and he twenty-five. She said he was the best bare-knuckle boxer in the whole of Ireland, and so feared because of his strength. Once, he had gone out looking for firewood with his faithful donkey called 'Wink', because it only had one eye. Poor Wink had problems with his feet as one of his shoes fell off, making it difficult for the one-eyed bandit to walk, so Grandad picked the donkey up, put him on his shoulders and carried him five miles home without breaking a sweat.

They had five sons, of which my father was one, and two daughters. Once four of his sons were old enough, he made them join the Irish Army; not that he was loyal to his country, he just wanted to get rid of them. As for his daughters, it had been down to Grandma to teach the girls to clean, cook, and look after babies. Grandad believed that if they had some kind of skills, maybe they'd be lucky enough to find husbands for themselves because they weren't blessed in the beauty department. She said he could be nasty at times, hence why she had come to stay with us for a while.

One day, Grandma asked if we would show her where the vet was because poor Bimbo was scratching the flesh off his skinny body.

The vet said: "What have we got here?"

"It's a dog, you *amadan*." (Meaning simpleton, or idiot in Gaelic.)

He said he could see it was a dog, but why was it wearing glasses?

"He is partially blind without them... he bumps into everything," she replied.

The vet took Bimbo's glasses off, put him on the bed, and called him to come to him. The dog fell off the bed. Grandma called the vet all the cunts under the sun, screaming he had caused her precious pet brain damage or even killed him. The poor man was very concerned. He held Bimbo in his arms – he was as stiff as a board with his mouth wide open.

"I think he may have had a stroke," said the vet man, looking at the dog worryingly.

"You killed my dog!" said Grandma, with tears dripping from her eyes.

That was her signal for Martinlee, Keith and myself to become hysterical. We'd pretend we were crying and put our hands over our eyes. Of course, Keith had to take it a step further by throwing himself on the floor and banging his fist on it while singing 'Bimbo, Bimbo, where you gonna go?', Grandma's favourite song.

The beautiful blonde assistant kneeled down beside Keith and cuddled him and tried to explain that the dog wasn't dead; it was just in shock after the fall.

"Hold me tighter!" cried Keith without a tear in his eyes.

"Here we go again," Martinlee said to me. "Keith's got tits on his brain," as Keith put his head between her bosoms.

"You cheeky little git!" she said to him with a disapproving look on her face. Keith had a big smile on his. With all the commotion, no one had realised Bimbo was sat up licking his paw, as if nothing had happened.

Grandma ran over to the now stressed-to-death vet and threw her arms around his neck to give him a hug for saving her dog.

"You must have healing hands," she told him.

"I did nothing, Mrs Maguire," he said.

"I know you fecking haven't, you twit," she said very quietly under her breath so he couldn't hear her.

"How did he get into this poor state?" he asked.

Grandma explained that she'd found him roaming the streets. She felt sorry for the poor animal and took him to her home because she is a widow and was bringing up three children on her own with very little money. She couldn't afford to pay for any treatment for him and feed her babies as well, pointing at us as if we were her kids.

The vet man fell for her story about the dog, but I don't believe he did about us being her children. She looked too old to have children our age.

He gave Bimbo two injections, shoved a suppository up his arse, plus gave Grandma some flea shampoo to wash him in and cream for his mange. He even measured the dog's head for a small pair of glasses, saying Bimbo was blind in his right eye. He'd have them make up new glasses for free.

Grandma was delighted with our acting. She gave us sixpence each and half a biscuit to her dog for playing dead: a super-cute trick she had taught him. In time his fur grew back, and with his new spectacles that made his eyes look gigantic, now the dinlo dog looked like a deranged alien from outer space, I thought.

My Uncles

Two of Father's younger brothers came to stay for a few weeks, as if we weren't overcrowded enough. Uncle Oliver and Raphael were on army leave from the King's Own Scottish Borderers. They were still dressed in their army uniform and looked very elegant. I had not seen Uncle Oliver in many years, but at the back of my brain, there was something familiar about him.

Raphael said hello to me and asked what my name was, so I knew I had not met him before. He was quite small in height, unlike his two other brothers, who were very tall in comparison. You could tell he was his mother's son because he was the image of Grandma.

Uncle Oliver threw his army kit-bag open on the floor. He came bearing gifts – sweets for all his nieces and nephews, small bottles of perfume for my elder sisters, when the smell hit the air, I thought, *Yuck, that smells like piss*. There was a Swiss penknife for each of my two older brothers. My little body trembled at the sight of them. Uncle Oliver noticed my fear and asked if I was okay.

Father replied for me, saying that I disliked knives.

"All knives?" asked Oliver.

"No, just ones like them," Father said.

"Oh, sorry to scare you, our Bridie. Don't worry, no one's going to hurt you with them knives," said Uncle Oliver reassuringly. *If only he knew,* I thought!

"No, she's a little crazy. She's even frightened of her own shadow," Father said jokingly, giving me and my two brothers the evil eye, as if we would ever open our mouths about anything that had happened, we knew full well what would be coming to us once they had gone. Father already had his hand on his belt and I'd not even breathed yet, let alone spoke, and he was giving us them maniac stares of his.

I didn't see a lot of my uncles in the coming weeks. They only had limited time on leave from the army and wanted to enjoy every minute of it. Drinking and chasing women were on their menu day and night. Of course, my parents followed along with them. Free booze was flowing like a kitchen tap, and they didn't have to pay a penny for it, thanks to my two uncles' savings.

Every Saturday evening, when my parents were out, Grandma would pull the old tin bath from the backyard into the front room. She'd fill it up with the water she'd boiled on the old stove for our weekly dip, as she called it. She had no shame stripping off her clothes in front of our Nancy and me. For a small-framed person, she had the biggest titties we had ever seen. They hung like pears on her stomach.

"That's all right," she said. "You can laugh, but when ya get older, ya will only be too pleased to have whoppers like these!"

How right she was. When I was nineteen years old, I was so flat-chested, if my head was turned backwards, no one would notice the difference. I was so embarrassed I would put socks down my bra to give the impression I had big boobs. Sad to say, I wasn't blessed with Grandma's genes, after all, more's the pity.

The snow was thick and falling fast when I opened the front door to the stranger one night. "Is Faith here?" he asked.

"No," I replied. "You have to go to the church around the corner to get that," I said, closing the door in his face.

"Who the fuck was that?" Father yelled from his bedroom.

"Someone looking for Faith."

How was I to know the man was my Grandfather Pat looking for Grandma, considering I'd never met him and didn't know Grandma's name was Faith. I didn't know why Father was yelling at me. *I see dead people,* I thought, *I'm not bloody psychic.*

In the 1960s, it wasn't the done thing to call your parents or grandparents by their first names anyway, so it wasn't a big deal that I didn't know her name, plus it was scowled upon as rude and disrespectful to your elders if you called them by their first names.

Grandma didn't seem too happy to see her beloved husband.

Martinlee and I were earwigging at the kitchen door, listening to them having words. "Where's the pox-faced bitch you ran off with?" Grandma yelled.

Grandad was making a strange noise as if he was being strangled.

When Grandma opened the kitchen door, we expected to see him lying dead on the floor.

"You didn't kill him then," laughed Keith.

"More's the pity," came Grandma's reply.

I was quite disappointed in Grandad. He looked nothing like the big, strong man Grandma had described in her stories. He couldn't have been more than five feet two in height. His white hair with his pale skin made him look ghost-like. His toothless mouth reminded me of a toad that Martinlee and I found once. We hid it under my bed in a shoebox. He or she escaped, and that was the last we saw of Freddie the Toad.

My grandparents stayed with us for another month. They had sold their property in Ireland and bought a little bungalow in Oldham, Manchester.

Before they left, old drunken Father Murphy held a Sunday Mass to bless their happy reunion. St Vincent's Church was packed that evening with all the locals; most were only there for the free spread, if they were honest. I know I was, I recognised some of them. The two old spinsters who had the most sour-looking faces on this earth. The Spinster Sisters – that's what people called them – were in their late sixties. They always wore long black dresses and coats. Their large black hats looked too big for their little pin heads. Father Murphy seemed to be afraid of them, because every time they went near him, he grabbed hold of the crucifix that was hanging around his neck as if his life depended on it.

Mrs Chapman, who was very posh, believed she and her husband Dennis were the only ones in the church without a blemish of sin in their lives. Unbeknownst to the cranky woman, her righteous husband was having an affair with Mrs Delaney. Mother said she'd seen him coming out of her home three or four times this week alone with his shirt hanging out of his trousers when he was supposed to be working. I'd overheard Mother telling Spotty Nora Cooper the gossip.

"Well what do you think of that, Betty?" asked Spotty Nora Cooper.
"Can you believe it?" said Mother. "Mrs Doyle said, 'Poor Mr Delaney, him with that big hump on his back and bent over like a camel. The dirty whore has worn him out with her demands for sex.'"

Nora Cooper stood listening to Mother's gossip with her spotty eye lids glued to Mother.

"I wouldn't take any heed what that Jessica Doyle is saying. Did you see how short she wears her dresses? You can see the fat cheeks of her arse rubbing together. A proper *gammy lakin* (dirty woman), if you ask me. I'd keep an eye on her with your John Paul, Betty. You know what a womaniser he is, and her a widow an' all," said Spotty Nora.

Father Murphy staggered to the altar, looking more drunk than usual. He seemed unsure why he was dressed in his robes, let alone what he was doing, standing at the altar with a bottle of red wine in his hand.

"Didn't we drink the wine with the Holy Communion this morning?" he asked Sister Joseph, who looked embarrassed by his question.

"No!" shouted out Spotty Nora, who happened to be sitting in front of her archenemy, Catherine McManus. "You drank it, Father!" she said with a crooked smile on her face.

111

The congregation burst into fits of laughter, except Catherine McManus, who reached over and grabbed Spotty Nora's hair, saying: "You fucking prostitute! How dare you talk to the holy father in that way!"

All punches were let loose between the two women. Spotty Nora managed to climb over the church pew, ripping at McManus' blouse. She was wearing no brassiere, and one of her fat titties popped out.

My brother Keith nudged me and said, "Look at the size of that, our kid!"

Hearing this, Grandfather Pat looked around. On seeing the woman's giant tit, he let out a cry. "Wow!"

Grandma took offence to see the delight on her husband's face and punched the side of his head in anger.

"Why did you do that?"

"I did nothing. It's not my fault her tit is looking in my direction, is it?"

And all the while, with all the usual drama kicking off, I just sitting there looking at my dear little granddad, wondering how on God's earth the man carried a donkey on his back. The mind boggled.

By now the two fighting women were rolling in the aisle and slapping the faces off each other. Sister Maria and Sister Margaret were doing their best to separate them.

"Ladies, ladies! Please, not in the House of God," said one of the nuns.

"Oh, Mother of God, Nora, you are disgracing yourself! The whole congregation and poor Father Murphy don't want to see you naked," said Sister Margaret.

My father's eyes were popping out of their sockets with the sight of Nora's red undergarments.

"Close your mouth! You're dribbling, you fecking eejit!" Mother told him, as she flipped one of his ears.

"Well now…" With that Father drew back and slapped mother bang in her face. At that moment the whole church erupted. Everyone who had a grievance against someone – uncles, nephews, cousins – was punching and kicking, ripping one another's hair out, some men exchanging blows. It was absolute chaos, but us kids loved it.

The police were called to separate them.

Drunken Father Murphy was sitting on the floor near the altar finishing off another bottle of red wine. He wasn't fazed by what was going on in his church. The irony was that he had seen it many times before in the ten years he had worked in the parish. "At least no one was ever murdered," he would say. He knew that the following Sunday we'd all be on our knees begging God and Father Murphy for forgiveness.

The nuns helped the police to clear the church of the people. No one was arrested. The nuns put it down to six of one, half a dozen of the other.

My poor grandparents never did get the blessing, not that Grandma was bothered. As she said, we had a laugh.

My brothers Martinlee and Keith and I were asked to stay behind to help the nuns tidy up the church for Sunday services. We gladly obliged, only because the big spread they had laid on hadn't been touched, and since there was no one left to eat the food, only the three of us, the pickings were ours.

Old Sister Deanna, who looked like she was going to croak at any minute, packed chicken and fish paste sandwiches, an assortment of cakes, and a few apples and oranges into large containers for us to take home to our family.

We didn't go home because we knew our parents would be rowing, because Father couldn't keep his eyes off Nora Red Knickers. So instead, we made our way to Piccadilly, devouring the food as we walked. What we had left over we gave to the tramps on the streets and some homeless people. Once we had finished doing our good deeds, we headed off to the pubs to do a bit of carol singing.

It was a week before Christmas, and people seemed to be more generous around that time of year, and folks were very merry. We sang 'Little Donkey' and 'Away in a Manger'. Well, some of it, we didn't know all the words. A hat was handed around for people to put money in for us in every pub we'd do the same routine. We made £10.

"We are millionaires!" said Keith.

We were really chuffed with ourselves and decided to spend some of the money on Christmas presents for each other. We knew we wouldn't be getting any from our parents or anyone else for that matter. The three separate orphanages we were in never obliged us with any gifts, as it was all about Jesus, not about giving. That Jesus must have got our birthday presents as well, because nothing ever showed up then either. We got nothing.

I bought Martinlee and Keith silver crosses and chains with Jesus' Mother Mary on them. Keith stole me a beautiful box of handkerchiefs with yellow roses on them: they were second to my favourite flower, lily of the valley. My mummy Sister Bernadette used to have a small jar of hand cream made from the pretty flower. She would let me use it all the time. I loved the smell of it because it reminded me of the times we had together. I still buy a bottle of it to this day.

We couldn't wait to get home to hide our presents underneath the floorboards with our new shoes, Nancy's unread books, and a little black doll we got for her.

We were glad when Father kicked us out of the house the next morning to do our daily chores of shoplifting and begging. Once outside, we made our way to our bombed house because we didn't fancy walking the cold streets of Manchester. Besides, we didn't need to. We had money left over from the night before. We gave Mother £3 and our sisters £1 for when we would all run away together.

My grandparents left for Oldham the next morning. I was sorry to see them go, especially Grandma. She was a very funny woman and always had me in fits of giggles. I grew to love her dearly and knew I would miss our weekly dip in the tin bath. My two uncles had gone back to the army a few days previously. The house felt cold and empty, even though it was still full of screaming children. I felt very emotional and wanted to cry over Grandma's parting, but in the madhouse, no one was allowed to show any emotion or anger. Only my parents had the privilege of showing any feelings, but I did howl and whinge for days in my bedroom where I couldn't be seen or heard by my parents.

Our Second Home the Bombed House

We had found an old tin dustbin sometime back. Martinlee had beaten it down to half its size with one of Father's hammers. He put small holes all the way around it, and we used it to do some cooking on. We had it standing on bricks that I had collected from the backyard. Under the bricks, we put a large metal tray which was also retrieved from the back, so we wouldn't set the house alight.

Martinlee struggled out in the deep snow to buy some food for us. Keith set about getting the fire going. He didn't have to look far for kindling – the bombed house was full of broken pieces of furniture.

The beautiful bright glow brought light and comfort to the damp room. Time was getting on, and Martinlee still hadn't come back. The snow was coming down very heavily, and the snowflakes looked as big as pennies.

Keith could see the worried look on my face and said: "Do you think he is buried up to his throat, under the snow and can't get out?"

"Don't be silly. You only get that amount in the mountains. This is bloody Manchester!" I replied.

Try as I might, I couldn't set aside my curiosity about our Martinlee's safety. What if he *was* under the snow screaming for help and no one could hear him? Even worse, he could turn into one of those abominable snowmen with red eyes and big teeth. He wouldn't be happy having to hide up for the rest of his life on his own. Keith and I couldn't go with him. *He'd probably eat us,* I thought.

"Come on, Keith," I said. "We'd best go looking for him."

As I crossed the room to retrieve my coat, I happened to glance out of the broken window. I could see Martinlee at the front door. He was smothered from head to foot with snow. His body was shaking violently as if he was doing one of his pretend fits. We helped him to get his wet clothes off and covered him with the bedding we had stolen off people's lines. Once he'd got some of my burnt bacon and eggs down him, he began to look human again. I put the pretty flowers he'd brought back with the food into the rusty tin that I used as a vase. There was a wooden drying rack that was hanging from the ceiling by ropes. I put Martinlee's wet clothes on it, hoping to get them dry before we made our way home. Finally, the three of us climbed into the smelly bed and believed all was well with the world and fell asleep.

As we entered the ugly house, we could hear screaming and yelling, a lot louder than usual.

"Act normal," Keith said as we made our way to the front room.

Father was lashing out with his belt at my sister Libby, calling her a dirty slag.

"What has she done wrong?" I asked Nancy.

"I think she has eaten someone's baby. It's none of our lot. I counted them, and they are all there," Nancy said.

"I wonder whose baby she has eaten," said Keith.

"It could be Bendy Wendy's. She just had one. Mother was telling Mrs Green next door the other day that she should get a larger hat to cover its face up. 'God, the child is ugly!' 'Oh, Betty, it's a sin to say cruel things about the little infant,' replied Mrs Green. 'Sin or not, she must have mated with a turkey. It frightened the fecking life out of me,' Mother said. Both of them were in fits of giggles," I said.

Father punched Libby in her face. She fell to the floor. She couldn't protect herself from the blows he rained down on her. She was begging him to stop. He pulled her up from the floor by her golden hair. Another punch to her stomach. She collapsed to her knees.

I ran to my sister's side to try and comfort her. A hard slap to my face knocked me sideways. Father raised his hand to hit me again. I sunk my teeth into his arm. I could taste his warm blood in my mouth, but still wouldn't let go. All my anger and frustration and hatred towards him went into my bite.

Mother ripped at my mouth with her fingers, trying to pry it open. A few more hard digs to my head, and I let go. Libby glanced over at me. Our eyes locked. The pain I saw in her beautiful blue eyes was heart-wrenching. Her face was covered in blood. She was holding onto the wall to keep her balance.

Father sat down on a chair. He seemed to be out of breath because of his tuberculosis disease. The doctor had warned him if he didn't stop drinking, he'd be dead in twenty years. The doctor was right...

Seeing as Father was visibly disoriented, I was feeling brave: I went to the back of the chair and dug my fingernails into his face, hoping to rip his skin from his face. Like he had scarred me for life, I was hoping to do the same to him.

Mother grabbed his belt and began beating the hell out of me with it, screaming, "How dare you attack your poor daddy, you little bastard!" She didn't stop until she was exhausted. "Get out of my sight! Get to your room!" she yelled at me as she gasped for breath.

I crawled up the stairs with every part of my body crying out in pain.

Martinlee and Keith took me into their bedroom. Blood was pouring from my lip and nose. The scar on my bottom lip from a previous beating had reopened. One of my brothers put a rag to my mouth to try and stop the flow of blood.

"Are you out of your mind? Jesus! When he gets his breath back, you are dead. I presume you know that?" Martinlee said.

"Not if we kill him first," Keith replied.

"How are we going to do that? Stick a poker up the bastard's hole?" Martinlee suggested.

"Maybe we can get the Mafia to do it for us," Keith said.

"The Mafia lives in Sicily, not bloody Manchester!" Martinlee said.

"How do you know that?" asked Keith.

"Because smart-arse Paul Jones who is obsessed about reading books about them said so."

"He didn't tell me that," said Keith, looking very upset because Paul was supposed to be his best friend at school and hadn't they made a pact not to keep secrets from each other?

"That spotty-faced cunt can go and kiss my arse from now on. I be telling him next time I'm at school, he is no longer a buddy of mine. The twat."

"How can that be secret if there are books about them?" Martinlee asked Keith.

"No matter. He can get lost anyway."

"Why don't you grow up, Keith!" Martinlee yelled.

"I'm taller than you!" cried Keith.

"Shush! Best we keep quiet in case we're overheard. Do you two want a beatin' as well? Once we get the opportunity to go to our bombed house, then and only then, we can put our brains together and work out how we're going to do the dirty deed on Father," I said.

Lying in bed that night, I cried so hard until my eyes were sore. I didn't know who I was whingeing over – Libby, myself or the whole damn situation that went on behind the closed doors of the ugly house. Why didn't Father seem to care what pain he inflicted on his daughters' bodies or minds? When you're a kid you kind of think it's normal, but then you grow up and the silent abuse you suffer as children has a long-lasting effect on all your lives. For me, it was self-loathing.

Playing Truant

My sister Kelly loved school. She had dreams of winning scholarships and going to college to become a doctor and work in hospitals.

Me, I hated it because I was constantly being shown up by the teachers and the other children because I couldn't read or write. So I was not as disappointed as Kelly when Father would tell her she couldn't go to school. There was a different reason for our absence – Kelly had to look after the young siblings and clean up the house, and I couldn't sometimes go because my bruises and cuts might be seen, and the last thing my parents needed was to have any authorities around the home because of me.

A few weeks after Christmas, Father received a letter from the court saying that he was summoned with his daughters, Kelly and me, because of our bad school attendance. My parents didn't seem too bothered about this. Mother said they'd probably get a fine and the judge could kiss her hairy arse for the money. The letter was thrown into the fire, and that was the end of the matter, until a week later, when the police turned up at our door to arrest them for not attending court that morning. Father explained that neither he nor his wife could read.

The police took them to the station and let them out on bail until the following morning.

Of course, we were well-prepared by our parents before we entered the court. My sister and I stood hand-in-hand, looking up at the judges – two men and two women. God, they had mean looks on their faces.

Kelly was asked to speak first, then me. I told the same story as she did: our parents had sent us to school every day, but we didn't like going so we bunked off without them knowing.

Next, our school files were read out:

"The children's absence from school is appalling. Out of the six months, since they were first signed into St Wilfred's School, the children only attended for three months. We visited the parents' home on many occasions, but unfortunately, no one was home," said the School Inspector, who had the biggest nose I'd seen on a human being.

My sister kept nudging me to stop looking at him, but I couldn't. I imagined myself having a sword fight with his very large nose. I let out a giggle. Another dig in my side from her.

Father and Mother were giving me dirty looks, but I couldn't help laughing.

The judges looked down at me with disapproval as I tried to control myself I suppose I should have taken the situation seriously, but as one of the judges said, I was only a child, what did I know? I didn't realise by the end of the day that my laughter would turn to tears.

The woman judge said if we promised her that we'd go to school, she would allow us to go home. If not, we would be taken away from our family and friends and put into care.

They asked me first, and I promised I would go.

I believed my sister Kelly was going to say the same, but she didn't. To my horror, she said she had no intention of going.

I looked at her in disbelief. "Please tell them you will go," I begged her, but she had already made up her mind. No way was she going back to the madhouse. She was very defiant and told the judges to send her away… and they did, right in front of my eyes too. Social Services were called into the room, took her arm, and led her away out of the court. I screamed after her to come back. She looked back at me with tears dripping down her face. The door closed behind her, and like a whisper, she had gone.

I was completely and utterly heartbroken. My best sister, whom I adored, had abandoned me. The sister who seemed to live in the shadows of the ugly house as if she was some kind of ghost and who very rarely spoke and had the kindest of hearts vanished in front of my eyes. If only beforehand she had told me her plan, I would have gone along with it, but now it was too late.

Martinlee, Keith and I were devastated that Kelly had gone. It was like she had died, and we were grieving her. The rest of the family carried on as if she never existed. No one ever spoke her name or talked about her. She had gone, so that was their attitude.

The only way we could cope with her absence was that I found a grave in Oldham Cemetery that looked like it had been abandoned and forgotten for years. Martinee and Keith and I pretended our sister Kelly was buried there. At least we told ourselves that we could come to the graveyard every other day to visit her. We would steal beautiful coloured flowers each week to put on the grave, and we'd spend hours sitting on the stone telling her about all the rows that were going on at home. Martinlee, Keith, and I were saving up every penny we could to travel the big world to find her, but for now, we were happy to imagine she was in the cold grave. At least we could visit her there, we understood what we were doing, we loved her so much and missed her more than she'd ever know.

We didn't tell anyone else in the family – they would have thought we were mad, but it helped to ease our pain to believe she was not too far away from us.

Looking back now, I don't blame her for wanting to get away from the beatings and half-starved children and her drunken, mad parents. She was offered a way out, and she took it.

I did see her once after she was taken away, in the flesh of course. I was thirteen years old in a children's home, and she came to visit us. It had been four long years since we had last seen her. I can't say I cried or showed any emotion toward her, because I had no tears or emotions left within me. The beatings and rapes and physical abuse had left me emotionally empty. I had by now shut down inside. Now, my only concern was with my younger siblings, who at this point were in the home with me.

Who's the Mother?

My two brothers and I came home from the bombed house. The children were a bit quieter than usual.

"I think we have come into the wrong house," Martinlee said jokingly. Our sister met us in the hallway.

"Has someone died?" I asked.

"No," came her reply.

"Mother is pregnant, and before you ask, Bridie, she didn't eat anyone's baby," said Ocean.

"How did it get into her stomach then?" asked Martinlee.

"Never you mind," said sister Ocean.

"Will Father try to kick it out of her belly like he did with Libby?"

"If he does, Bridie, don't you dare try and stop him," said Keith.

"Don't worry, I won't."

The days passed into weeks, then months. Sister Libby, who seemed to be very down, walked around the house as if she was in another world. Her blue eyes looked empty of any emotion; her beautiful face always looked pale and drawn and tired. The baby she didn't cough up was getting bigger in her stomach and was draining all of her strength. She wasn't allowed out of the house because of her pregnancy. She more or less was a prisoner in the ugly house.

Once her baby came into the world, my parents had plans to take custody of her child, which I don't think Libby was too happy with.

Libby would take responsibility of her child indoors, but wouldn't be allowed to take the baby out in public because my parents didn't want people to know that the child belonged to her. What added to her misery was that Jeremy, my older brother who our Libby was very close to, had left home; he'd got himself a new girlfriend. She turned up at the house one day on a motorbike, all dressed in leather. There was silver and black writing on her bike, but we couldn't read it, so Martinlee asked her what it said.

"That's the name of my motorbike, Harley Davidson."

"Emm, that's strange," said Keith. "She can't be all there in the head to have a name for her bike. Mind you you'd need to be backward to end up with Jeremy."

She told him to "Get lost, you little twat."

Jeremy came out of the house, jumped on the back of the motorbike, and raced off into the night, not to be seen for the next thirty years. That was at Mother's funeral.

Can't say I was that bothered when he left. To me, it was just one less mouth to feed. I imagine that sentiment goes against everything we are supposed to feel for a sibling. I suppose in my family it was like dog eat dog, and sometimes we were so hungry that if we'd had a dog, we would probably have eaten it. Jeremy sent Mother a letter saying that he had to go on a long journey to 'discover' himself.

"Thick cunt," Father said as he walked over to the fire and threw the letter into it.

"Mark my fucking words," Mother said, "he'll be back with his balls between his legs before we know it."

"I fucking hope not," came Father's reply.

I suppose I could see why Libby was upset at Jeremy's parting. She, Ocean and him were like The Three Musketeers – one for all and all for one. That kind of thing went on with the three of them. For the rest of us, we could have been invisible for all they cared. Libby sank into a very bad depression and spent most of her days in her bedroom. Father had hit her again. I wasn't in when it happened. I don't remember anyone letting me know what it was over. One night, Father yelled for Libby to come down from upstairs. She didn't reply. I found her dangling from the long beam in the centre of her bedroom ceiling. An old stocking was wrapped around her neck very tightly. Her face was red, and her lips blue.

I ran down the stairs screaming, "She's dead! She's dead!"

"Who is dead?" asked Ocean.

"Libby, she's murdered herself," I cried.

Father ran up to her with the rest of us following. He cut her down with a penknife, the same one he had cut me with, and laid her on her bed. She opened her eyes. They looked red and haunted. Her beautiful face resembled a death mask.

I was told to run and fetch some water. She drank a little bit, and the colour came back to her face. She tried to drink some more but complained her throat was sore.

"Go and make her some toast. That will help the muscles in her throat open up again."

I thought that was a strange request. Shouldn't I be running to fetch the doctor or ambulance for her? I did what I was told. Once I entered my sister's room again, Father left.

Libby was sitting up in her bed, crying her eyes out. She didn't want the burnt toast I had made, so I ate it: waste not, want not.

"Did he bring you back from the dead?" I asked her.

"He is not Jesus, Bridie," she said.

"I know that. If he was, good people would have murdered the pig a long time ago."

"I wish they had, instead of poor Jesus."

I insisted: "Why did you want to die?"

"To escape from *him*," she replied.

"You can, you can. Come with me to my secret garden," I said excitedly.

"Garden? What are you on about, our Bridie? Not another one of your silly dreams?" Libby said with her half-stretched larynx and croaky voice.

I could see she wasn't really interested in another one of my stories that I would tell our little brothers and sisters, but I continued rabbiting on anyways, probably just rambling on with nerves.

I told her about all the things that were in my garden; the land that ran for miles as far as the eye could see, the beautiful blue sea that had a rainbow completely covering it, the multitude of fruit trees… "But none of the children I see in my gorgeous garden eat the fruits."

"Why?" asked Libby.

"Because they never get hungry," I replied.

"Do you know the kids in your gardens?"

"No, I only meet them there, but my mummy, Sister Bernadette, is looking after them," I replied.

Libby's eyes were closed and she let out a sigh. I presumed she was asleep. As I was leaving the room, she said, "Bridie, promise me you will not tell anyone about what you see or think you see, because you will be put in a nuthouse."

I didn't know what kind of house that was.

She said I was a special kind, but I just dismissed her comment as I wasn't keen on peanuts anyway. Although I was quite surprised by her, that was the longest conversation she had ever had with me, even though I did most of the talking.

A week later, Libby gave birth to a healthy little boy who she called Paul. He was such a handsome fella, with his blue eyes, a mop of blonde hair and chubby cheeks. Looking at him he could have been Bible John's child. Bible John had got that name because he used to sell bibles around the neighbourhood houses. Father bought one from him. It was £3, but he had only to pay two shillings a week until it was paid for because he was friends with Father.

He was a handsome-looking man: blonde hair and brown eyes. Father said he was a catch for any good girl. There were rumours he was going out with my sister Libby and he was the father of her baby, so Father said, but I didn't believe this was true at that time. It was just a cover-up for the neighbours if it got out that she was having a baby and to stop them asking any questions. Father put all the children's names in the big Bible book. He had so many he couldn't remember some of them and had to be reminded of them.

Paul was a quiet child, and it was very rare for him to wake up during the night. If he did, Libby would be called to attend to his needs. He wasn't allowed to sleep in the same room as her. He slept downstairs in my parents' bedroom. She was not even allowed to take him outside the house. Mother had lost the baby she was carrying. The news was kept within the family circle on Father's orders.

Mother told all the neighbours, and anyone who wanted to listen to her, that Paul was her child. One woman who lived on our street said Mother should stop having kids because she already had thirteen kids that she doesn't or can't look after. Mother punched her in the face. The police were called, and Mother was taken to court and fined £5.

Another New Baby

Baby Paul was a year old when Mother announced to the rest of the family that she was three months gone with child. We didn't know what she was talking about, but the other adults weren't smiling, so my brothers Martinlee and Keith guessed the news must be bad.

Martinlee said, "Maybe she is gone with baby Paul."

"How can she be gone when she and the baby are still here?" I replied.

"I think what she is trying to tell us is, she is fucking off with him in three months' time," said Keith.

God, I was so jealous of Keith's wisdom. He was so smart, and everything he would say to Martinlee and me made perfect sense to us.

One day we were playing out in our street, swinging from a lamp post that Keith had tied a rope around. Baby Paul was in the big old silver cross pram that one of my brothers stole from someone's backyard. It was quite rusty, but once Father cleaned it up, it looked as good as new.

Two girls looked in the pram. One said to the other, "Look, another dirty pikey."

Martinlee said, "I may be that, but good looking with it, unlike you with your ugly cow's face."

The girl pulled Martinlee's hair and tried to wrestle him to the ground. Both ended up rolling on the ground. The other girl, seeing that her friend was losing the fight, joined in the fight, so Keith jumped on her back and ripped her blouse. Her small titties popped out.

"Wow!" laughed Keith. "Can I cuddle them?"

The poor girl was so embarrassed and ran up the street trying to cover herself up, with Keith running after her asking for another peek. Yes Keith was clever, but he was also titty-mad.

Keith and Titties

One night Martinlee, Keith and I were out begging for money. Two pretty women in their twenties passed by us. Keith shouted out at one of them to show him her titties.

"You bloody rude little cunt! I'll give you a good smack on your arse if you say that again."

Keith beamed and pulled down his trousers, exposing his arse and calling after them.

"Bejesus! Grab that bastard, Ellie! I'll wipe the floor with him."

He took off running up the high street with his pants around his ankles. It was hilarious. Even the women couldn't help laughing at him and gave me sixpence.

"I don't know what it is with him and women's breasts," I said to our Martinlee.

Martinlee put his behaviour down to the nuns in the boys' orphanage that they were both in Ireland. "They deprived him of titty affection."

"What does that mean?" I asked Martinlee.

"Well," he said, "he was put in the home when he was a baby, and I don't think the nuns have titties, and they are bald. He didn't take to a bottle, so I think he was fed with rubber gloves. I have seen a farmer once who worked in our orphanage fill up one of them with goat's milk and feed a baby sheep with it from the glove. Keith was probably fed that way as well."

"So he thinks all women's tits are like rubber gloves... something to get food from?"

"You know him, always talking about food and how he is starving."

"So, that's why he is titty-mad?" I said.

"Yes, definitely," Martinlee replied.

"You said the nuns were bald... What has that got to do with all of this?"

"Nothing," he said.

In late November, Mother had a baby boy. She called him Michael. He was gorgeous, with jet black hair and bright, piercing blue eyes. Mother said he reminded her of Paul Roy, the little boy she lost years back.

It was like a lightbulb was switched on in my brain. Memories came flooding back to me. The tents, wagons, and of course me putting black boot polish on Paul Roy's head to make him look as if he had hair.

I took myself down to our rat-infested cellar and cried my heart out for the loss of my brother, who I truly loved, along with the loss of Sister Bernadette (my mummy). I was so young and felt emotionally so alone; I was still having to deal with Father abusing my little body as and when he pleased. I didn't know how one's eyes could hold so many tears. How long I cried for I don't know, but I was feeling exhausted when the tears stopped.

My sister Ocean was confined to bed on doctor's orders. She'd had rickets as a child and had one leg longer than the other, which caused her tremendous pain at times. She had to wear a metal brace on her right leg, which she detested.

"She needs to rest her leg up for a couple of weeks before her operation," the specialist told Mother upon his visit to our madhouse. "A few weeks off work will help the swelling of her joints to go down."

"Don't you worry, Dr Finley, I'll make sure she doesn't lift a finger… or a leg, comes to that," Mother said jokingly.

The old doctor found Mother's comment very amusing. He burst out laughing and said, "Oh, Mrs Dublin, you should have been a comedian!"

"How dare you call me a fool, you drunken old bastard! I could smell the gin on your breath a mile away, you old crooked-eyed cunt," Mother screamed at him.

The doctor raised his thick eyebrows and fixed them on her. "I'm sorry, Mrs Dublin, if you think I insulted you," he said with embarrassment. "I was giving you a compliment on your sense of humour."

"You can't be going around giving compliments to married women. If my John Paul heard what you said, God knows what he would do to you."

Ocean covered her head with a few coats; I could see she was laughing, her shoulders were going up and down like a yo-yo.

Dr Finlay looked completely confused as he left our madhouse. No sooner had he gone, Mother told Father that the old quack fancied her.

"He's probably on the gin again," came his reply.

His comment didn't faze Mother, it only put a smile on her face for the rest of the day, thinking Father's remark came out of jealousy.

Sergeant Ian Brady

It was a cold, bitter day. Keith was too tired to go begging and decided to rest up in our bombed house for the day. Martinlee and I planned to meet up with him in the park near Alexandra Road in the evening. After sitting in the cold for about two hours waiting for Keith to show up when he didn't, we made our way home, believing he was probably there. He wasn't.

And when the clock struck ten, Martinlee and I were really concerned. Keith wouldn't stay out that late on his own. Something bad must have happened to him. We decided we'd best go out looking for him. Our parents were still out drinking; our older siblings didn't give a toss if we were in or out. Their concern was with the young ones. They had no interest in me or Martinlee and Keith. Sometimes I wondered if they even realised we existed. I don't ever remember having a full conversation with my two older sisters or my older brothers – well, unless I was doing all the talking. I've got to admit, I was a chatterbox, and I perceived it probably got on their nerves at times. A bit of acknowledgment now and then wouldn't have hurt them, I thought.

Martinlee and I walked the three miles back to Piccadilly Circus, hoping to find Keith in one of our hideouts. There was no sign of him anywhere, plus the other beggars and tramps hadn't seen him.

"I don't understand. He's never away from us. Do you think someone has murdered him?" Martinlee said.

"He's not a fucking eejit! He's too clever to be murdered, but something is very wrong. I can feel it in my belly," I said.

We made our way home, praying to all the saints, Jesus, Mary, Joseph and Mother's favourite, lily of the valley, to bless Keith and bring him home safe.

"We don't know anything about that saint," Martinlee said. "She must have lived in Wales, because that's the only place on earth where there were valleys."

I told him I didn't care where she lived, as long as she hears our prayers and brings him back to us.

Sister Ocean said she hadn't seen Keith since that morning, and how comes he wasn't with us?

Martinlee lied and said he'd been in one shop and us in another. "Maybe he took a long way home," I said.

Time was ticking on. It was dark and still no sign of him. My parents were out and didn't know he was missing, and if they had, they wouldn't have given a shit anyway.

My biggest fear was the policeman who had pulled us up and accused us of stealing from school some months back had arrested him for something. I wasn't attending school on that day, because Father said he needed me at home to help out with the children. I had made arrangements to meet up with my brothers after school in the wasteland near our home.

I hung about for some time and wondered if they had forgotten or gone off stealing without me until I'd heard Keith calling my name. They ran straight across the main road without looking. Cars were beeping at them from all directions. *God,* I thought, *now we are in for it.* A young police officer came towards us. We knew most of the police in our area this one was new to us.

"Well, well," he said. "What do we have here? Been stealing, have we?"

"No, we ain't!" I cried.

Keith was keeping his eyes low to the ground.

"We were looking for our sister," Martinlee told him.

"What are your names?"

Martinlee was the Lone Ranger, Keith was Tonto, and I decided to call myself the Queen for no particular reason.

"And your name?" I asked him boldly.

"Sergeant Ian Brady," came his reply.

Can't say his name meant anything to us at that time.

He had found a Mickey Mouse watch in our Martinlee's trouser pocket that he believed Martinlee had stolen, which he had. The policeman said he had to arrest Martinlee.

Grabbing Martinlee by the scruff of his neck, he told me and Keith to get lost. We wouldn't budge, not until the Black Maria turned up to take him.

"He's not going in one of them; he's going in that white van."

A woman was sitting in the driver's seat of the van with a small white dog jumping up and down towards the window. The woman had a black scarf covering some of her blonde hair, only her fringe was visible, and she wore a dark coat or cardigan. What was strange to me was that she was wearing black shiny gloves to drive, considering it wasn't that cold.

There was something about the way she looked at me that sent a chill all over my body, and a voice in my head said *run.*

But I couldn't.

Sergeant Ian Brady was dragging our Martinlee to the van, as Martinlee was calling him all the cunts under the sun.

I ran at the police offer and kept kicking him in the back of his legs until one of his legs buckled under him. He let go of our Martinlee to grab a hold of me.

I ran around the white van to escape his clutches. He screamed out at the woman to catch me.

As she got out of the van, Martinlee and Keith began picking up stones and throwing them at the pair of them. One large stone hit the window screen, and it smashed to two pieces.

"That will hold you cunts," Martinlee yelled, as both boys ran off in one direction and me in another.

The three of us arrived home safely. We never mentioned our run-in with the law in case we got a beating from our parents, especially if they knew that we had attacked him and pelted his van with stones.

My brothers and I agreed that if we ever saw Ian Brady again, we would run like greyhounds. If we were caught, we didn't speak English. Keith would play deaf and Martinlee blind and mute. As for me, I would be my brother's carer and only speak my native tongue of Irish Gaelic. With our plan in hand, we never gave the incident another thought, until tonight.

We made our way home once again, hoping Keith would be home. He wasn't.

Sister Libby told us to get to bed. She offered us a slice of bread and dripping each. We declined, our stomachs too sick with worry.

Eventually, Keith arrived home. I wanted to kill him but was relieved to see him.

His face looked full of fear. His breathing was shallow and panicky. Once he'd settled down, he told us what had happened to him.

He had met a woman in the park who had offered him some bread and jam to eat. Without a thought he accepted as he was so hungry, He had paid no attention to how she looked or even asked her name, he could just taste the jam on his tongue, no surprise there. He "loved his grub," so he agreed to go with her to her house.

On reflection he said he wasn't quite sure, but he thought it was the same woman who tried to grab me previously. Me and our Martinlee both gasped a shocked breath. Was that Brady policeman there too? Was it Brady and the same blonde woman?

"Why would a policeman and this woman take you to their home, not the police station?" asked Martinlee.

"I don't know," Keith said. "She offered me bread and jam. I was hungry, so I followed her home. Then that Brady appeared out of nowhere."

Keith said he had heard them rowing and got scared, plus the woman's attitude towards him changed. Her gentle voice had turned harsh as she slammed the pieces of bread and jam on the table for him to eat.

He said he'd got a queer feeling in his stomach and knew he had to get out of there fast. He had decided to leg it out the window but as he tried to get out, he realised it would only push up so far. He kept pushing and pushing until he finally got it open enough to squeeze his thin body through, but Brady managed to grab one of his feet. Thank God Brady wasn't strong enough to pull him back in, as Keith kept kicking at him with his free leg. Once out of the house, he ran home without stopping.

The three of us decided not to tell a soul about what had happened to us, because we were frightened we would get into trouble. Who were we kidding? We should have been more frightened of the realisation that no one actually cared. We decided never to go into other people's houses, which was something we often did for a piece of cake and a cup of warm, milky tea that nice folks would give us because they pitied us. We never spoke about the matter again and prayed we would never bump into Sergeant Ian Brady again.

It wasn't until quite some time later, when we were talking to our favourite hairy hotdog man in Piccadilly Centre, that we learned the truth.

"They got him, I see."

"Who got who?" Keith asked, looking at our friend, puzzled.

"The cunt," he said, picking up the local *Echo* newspaper and pointing at a picture on the front page. "Brady and his whore…" he continued to say, "…killing them poor children, burned them on the Moors, they did."

Seeing their faces in the news put a look of horror on our little faces.

"Jesus!" Martinlee said. "That's the policeman and the blonde woman who tried to arrest us!"

Keith was trembling from head to toe and put down the free hotdog our friend had given him a few seconds before showing us the newspaper.

"Are you all right, my boy?" asked the greasy hotdog man. "Got a ticky belly, have you?"

Keith couldn't speak. He looked like he was so shocked, literally dumbfounded. Martinlee and I led him away from the stall by his arm and said our goodbyes to our hairy buddy. We walked the three miles back to our bombed house without speaking a word to each other. Once inside, we laid Keith down on the dirty mattress. He fell asleep instantly.

Martinlee said, "You realise Keith could have been one of them children who them bastards killed? So could have we."

"Yes, you are so right, Brother Martinlee, Thank the Blessed Lord our Keith survived the evil pair," I replied.

Martinlee agreed with me and said, "I think he should have the number six as his lucky number."

I pulled a face at him. "What are you talking about?"

"Well, he could have been the sixth kid to be killed by them, and can't you see, Bridie? He's the only survivor."

"My God! I didn't realise that," I cried. "Well, if he's on six, then he'd better be careful, even a cat's only got nine lives."

"I'll make you right," nodded Martinlee in agreement. Even more shocking, our kid left a free hotdog.

The Runaways

My sister Libby and Ocean ran away from home. Father spent a few days looking for them, eventually returning home with Ocean and Libby's baby Paul, but no sign of Libby.

I couldn't understand how he managed to get Paul off his mother. She adored her son. He was her life. Why did she hand him over so quickly? Where was she? Did he kill her in a rage of temper? Question after question flooded my mind, but no one was willing to assure me she was okay.

A few days later, Father cut Ocean's beautiful long black hair, telling her she should think twice before running away again.

It was horrible to see my sister sobbing her eyes out as he chopped away at her hair, leaving her head almost bald.

My own hair was quite short, so was the rest of the children's because we were prone to catching nits and lice. It didn't worry us, but Ocean was a young woman. Her appearance was important to her. She kept herself prim and proper for work. The factory she worked in was full of young men around her age of sixteen and over, so of course she wanted to look her best, hoping she would catch one of their eyes. Whether she did or not, I don't know. Even with her semi-bald head, she was still very pretty.

The next morning Father sent her back to work. That was fifty-three years ago. She never returned home, and that was the last any of us ever saw of her.

I can understand why they had to escape the madhouse, but what I didn't understand was, why leave me and our sister Nancy, knowing Father was sexually and physically abusing us?

I prayed night after night that they would come and rescue us, or maybe one of them would go to the Social Services or the police to report my father. They did nothing to help us. I felt they'd completely abandoned us. *Why?* I asked myself.

By them not seeking help for us once they had their freedom, Father was allowed to carry on abusing our little bodies. We lived in fear every night, and there was no one there to help us. Our two younger brothers did their best to protect us, but there was only so much they could do.

One night Father came home from one of his drinking binges without Mother again. He was roaring drunk, shouting for me to come downstairs. My legs wouldn't move properly with fear.

Terrified, my little sister Nancy cried, "Please don't let him hurt us again."

I tried to assure her I wouldn't let him near her. How I was going to achieve this task, I had no idea.

Brothers Martinlee and Keith came to our rescue. My sister and I followed them down the stairs, praying the wooden stairs wouldn't squeak as some of the floorboards were loose. Martinlee rebuked Nancy, whispering to her to shut up crying. If we were caught, we'd all be in for a fecking beating. I had to put my hand over her mouth to block out the sobbing noise she was making.

We knew Father was in his bedroom because he was coughing his lungs up. He was told to stop his drinking. If he didn't, he'd be dead by the age of fifty. His tuberculosis wasn't getting any better because of drink. He didn't seem to care what the doctor was telling him.

Once we reached the kitchen back door, we ran down the long alleyway. I couldn't believe our luck – we'd managed to escape his clutches for one night.

It was still raining. The sky was pitch black, and the cold wind stuck our little white cotton dresses to us like a second skin. We kept running down the silent streets, blinded by the rain. I had no idea where to go to get out of the rain. We were too far away from our bombed house for Nancy's little legs to run that far.

I spotted a police car and thought it could be that Sergeant Ian Brady. I knew he was locked up, but it didn't stop me from thinking, *What if he had escaped from prison?* We ran behind a red brick wall and hid under unkempt thorn bushes. The ground was freezing, and as the wind blew stronger, I felt like it was eating away at every bone in our bodies. I knew we couldn't stay there all night. Nancy was complaining that her shoeless feet were hurting her, but there was nothing I could do about it.

I only had one option: go to Bible John's house. Bible John's family were working-class people. His dad and brother had passed away some years back. It was just him and his mother, who doted on him. Even though he was twenty-three years old, his mum still packed his sandwiches for his lunch. I didn't like him very much – something about him just didn't feel right. I felt a bit like a hypocrite going to his home for some kind of help, but we were desperate.

I could see his house still had lights on, so I knocked. His mother opened the door. "Oh, dear Jesus!" she cried. "John, dear, please come down here."

"Who is it, Mother, at this time of night?" we could hear him yelling at her.

"I don't know, dear. Two little girls without shoes on are asking for you."

"Bloody hell," John said. "Come in."

We followed him and his mum into the front room. "Do you know these children, dear?" she asked.

John's mother left the room to make some sweet tea for us all.

"What are you doing out at this time of night? Where are your coats and shoes? Has something happened at home? Do your parents know you are running the streets like feral children?"

I had no idea what he meant by that. The man wouldn't shut up and let me answer any of his questions.

His mother brought in tea and cake. Nancy's eyes couldn't stop staring at it. John's mother asked should she make up some beds for us for the night.

"No thanks, Mother; I am taking them back to their parents, who I expect are probably worried out of their minds over them."

"How can the parents not know their children are not tucked up in bed safely, dear?"

"Not to worry, Mother. I will deal with this. You go to bed."

Nancy began crying. She didn't want to go home. I wanted to tell this kind-faced woman why we took flight in the first place but didn't think she would believe us if I did, so I kept my mouth shut.

Once inside his van, I was hoping to share our troubles and suffering that Father was putting on us, that and our mother knew the torture we had to endure with or without her being around.

Once he started to preach to me about how good our parents were, hoping he would find compassion in his heart for us went out the window. It very quickly dawned on me, there was no way he would believe us and not take us back home. Instead we just sat there listening to how great John thought our parents were and how they struggled to bring up their very large family and how our poor father had tuberculosis which had stopped him from working for so long, and our poor mother so upset over her miscarriage a few weeks back. Considering my youngest brother was only six months, it must be very hard for her, without her worrying over not having enough food to feed them all.

I didn't tell John that I was with Mother when she miscarried the baby. I was ordered by Father to wash away the blood that was running down her legs, but at that time, I didn't know what a miscarriage was. I had it in my head that Father had cut her with a knife, and that's why she was bleeding so much until the ambulance man told Father that she had lost the child.

John continued to tell me that Father was devastated over the loss of his child, and with my sisters running off, causing my poor parents unnecessary stress, it was no wonder Mother had lost her little baby.

Father forgot to tell John that he was raping his girls and that's why they had run away, and a few days before Mother lost the baby, he and she were so pissed they got rowing as usual and lashed out at each other, and it was Father's attack on Mother that had killed the child, not the so-called stress of my big sister runaways.

Once outside our home, John prayed and asked God to make us all good children and help us to be proud of our parents.

"Remember, Bridie," he said, "The Bible says 'Honour thy father and mother,' so off you go now, be good and do as you're told."

I thought if he had to fight to live every day of his life with parents like ours, he wouldn't be saying that.

Father opened the door. He was taken aback, seeing his friend standing there with his kids in tow.

"Oh, God, John! I didn't know they were missing! They must have sneaked out without me knowing."

I saw the worried look on Father's face wondering if we had spilt the beans on him.

"Get to your bed," he ordered us.

Martinlee, Keith and myself were listened from the top of the stairs, trying to work out the next move in case Father the maniac was coming up after us, but he was too busy playing Saint Father at the front door, spinning his yarns, saying Mother had left him again and taken all the children's food money with her, and him not being well enough to work an' all. How in good God's name was he going to manage to feed his poor children?

"I hate to ask you for money, my friend, as I already owe you money for the Bible."

"Forget about what you owe," said John, as he brushed a strand of his blonde hair from one side of his forehead to the other, handing over ten shillings and promising to bring some food over for us in a few days' time.

"What a dickhead," Brother Martinlee said. "Why can't he see Father is having him on?"

"He's a Christian," said Keith. "I don't think they are allowed to see bad in anyone."

John said his farewell to Father, who took himself off to bed.

Nancy and I slept under my brother's bed for safety, just in case he came looking for us. It was very cold, the wooden floorboards were freezing. We only had a few old coats to put over us, but at least we felt safe hiding.

Mother came back the next morning, and nothing was said about us ending up in Bible John's house.

A couple of nights later, she was gone again after having a blazing row over some woman. Mother accused him of sleeping with Queenie. Everyone knew her in Hulme, Collyhurst and Moss Side. She was a prostitute and not a pretty one at that. She was five feet tall and wore tons of makeup. Her rotten teeth were always stained with red lipstick. Keith believed she was a he-she, because of her large Adam's apple that poked out from the middle of her turkey-like neck.

Martinlee asked: "Where did she get her big tits from if she's a man?"

Of course, as usual, Keith had the answer for us, saying he had seen pictures of men who were half-man and half-horse, so she must be half-woman, half-man… top end woman, bottom half man. "I wish I had tits." Keith said, "I'd play with the day and night."

Brother Keith was so clever, I thought, wishing I had the wisdom he was blessed with. "So, if she was dying to go to the toilet, which one do you think she'd use?" I asked.

"The man's one because she got a dick."

I asked her one day which bits of herself she sold. "All of me," came her reply.

We couldn't understand why Mother would be jealous of Queenie. She must have been a hundred years old and stank like a pole cat, whatever one of them smells like; if it's shit, then I'd be right.

We had no idea where Mother had gone, but Father was blaming me and Nancy for her absence again. He came into our bedroom and told us to fecking take our clothes off. We refused, which made him mad at us. He beat us with his belt until we both stripped. He began punching the hell out of us. We tried to protect ourselves with our mattress, but it was too heavy for us to keep up against our little bodies. Sister Nancy's face was covered in blood. She fell to the floor, her eyes closed and her mouth opened as if she was trying to scream, but nothing was coming out of it. Father was trying to rape her. I jumped on his back, pulling at his hair to stop him hurting her. He stopped, turned around, and punched me so hard in the face that I fell backwards and hit my head against the wall.

That's all I remember.

When I came around, lots of strange faces were kneeling down beside me. A woman told me I was safe now. I pushed her away from me, yelling, "Where's my sister Nancy?"

A policeman put his hand out to grab my arm, stopping me from trying to reach out to my sister. They didn't know if she was dead or alive as they struggled to get her down from the chimney. Believing he had killed her, Father had tried to hide her body up there; only her legs were dangling down from the chimney when thankfully, with the grace of God, the police arrived as if the blessed Lord had sent them Himself to save our little lives..

She was covered in black soot when they got her down. Her eyes were closed, her body limp. The ambulance man was pounding on her chest and breathing into her mouth. I thought he was trying to rape her as well. Taking the oxygen mask off my face, I shouted at him to stop hurting her; then I blacked out again.

My head was hurting badly. I couldn't distinguish where I was. Bright lights caused my eyes to ache. Maybe I was in Hell. After all, Sister No Legs would tell us kids that people who hated others would go there, and I hated my father. I wouldn't have been surprised if her God had sent me there. I didn't feel any fire consuming me, so I couldn't be there.

I tried to get up, but my body wouldn't do what my brain was asking it to do.

A thin figure in white walked towards me. I asked, was I in Heaven or Hell, and "Where is my little sister?"

"No," said the voice, "You are in intensive care."

I don't remember the nuns telling me about this place, I thought.

"My name is Holly. I am one of the nurses who'll be looking after you."

"So, I am in hospital then?"

"Yes."

"Why can't I open my eyes properly?"

"They are quite swollen at the moment. Nothing to panic over."

"What have you lot done with my sister Nancy?" I demanded to know.

"She's doing well," said the nurse. "You'll be able to see her in a few days. Now rest."

Normally I would have put up a fight and demanded there and then to see her, but I felt so weak and believed what the nurse told me.

I was taken to a ward where my sister was after a week. She was black and blue, but alive. We hugged each other and cried. Some of the doctors and nurses were crying as well.

One night we were looking out of the hospital window. A sly fox with a large bushy tail came out from behind a tree. After doing a quick tour of the lawn, it ran behind some bushes. Nancy had never seen one before. She wanted us to go and find it so she could have it as a pet. Was she kidding, I said. We'd end up eating the poor thing.

I said I would get her a toy instead. I stole her a lovely teddy bear from the lost property box in the hospital. I didn't think whoever had mislaid it would have begrudged her having it. She absolutely loved it.

The police came to see us in the hospital and said Father was on remand in prison for beating us, and I being the oldest one would have to appear in court as a witness against him. I didn't want to do it but had no choice.

Mother had to take myself and Nancy back to the hospital to have our stitches taken out. I had eighteen in my head and three in my lip. Nancy was fortunate enough to escape with just a few.

It had been three weeks since the attack, and Nancy was still coughing. She had to have another lung test and see the lung specialist because she had sniffed a lot of black soot from the chimney into her little lungs. The doctor was concerned her lungs were damaged.

Mother didn't give a feck what he was telling her about Nancy's illness. She wasn't happy with the long wait. All she was concerned about was that her friends had paid for some gin and tonics for her and had put them in the woods so she could get them down her throat. She had promised Father she would lay off the drink until he came out of prison. She was getting angrier by the minute. My sister Nancy and myself wouldn't forget to tell the untrue story that mother had invented: we had to convince the court, police and hospital, about how our sister Libby had attacked us and not father.

"It wasn't your fecking father that beat you… do you little bastards hear me?" How could we not? She pumped it into our heads about thirty times a day.

Poor Nancy said, "It was Father, Mummy, not our sister Libby. You must be forgetting, she ran away and wasn't there."

A hard slap across her face got her crying. The doctor asked her why she was so upset.

Mother answered the question for her. "She is frightened of hospitals. She'll be okay, won't you, dear?" Mother said.

Nancy was given another appointment to attend the hospital again in six weeks for another X-ray and was given an asthma pump to help her breathe better.

I was discharged, but had to take antibiotics for the chest infection I had, but nothing for the big yellow bruises that covered my entire body.

I held my sister's hand on the long walk back to the ugly house and wondered if we would be fortunate enough for the courts to take us all away from Mother.

The day came to go to the court. The police said Nancy was too young to be a witness, but I still had to go.

I was called in. I was terrified. The court was full, with faces I didn't know. Four men were sitting behind a large bench. I thought maybe they were related to one another because they all had long white curly hair that looked like a sheep's hair and black coloured robes.

I followed the policeman to the witness box. I was told to stand on the stool so I could be seen by all. The judge in the middle asked me my name and how old I was.

"I am nine, mister."

He told me not to be afraid and would I tell him what had happened to me and my sister Nancy. I remembered Mother's threatening words: "Feck it up, and I kill you myself." So I lied.

I was trembling with fear, and my teeth were chattering as I spoke.

"My sister hit us with a knife…" Why I said a knife, I don't know… "And she pushed our Nancy up the chimney."

I looked over at my father. He was smiling at Mother. I couldn't understand why I had to be in the same room as him.

"Are you telling us the truth, Bridget?"

I shook my head to his question, then I vomited everywhere in the witness box and on the stool. I was taken outside to get some air.

The court was adjourned until my mess had been cleaned up.

Mother lit up a cigarette. Her hand was shaking as she put it in her mouth. I watched the grey haze of smoke disappear into the atmosphere, wishing I could do the same.

Father got eighteen months for cruelty to his children.

My sister Nancy and I were never examined at the hospital to see if we were sexually assaulted, so his secret was kept safe from the court.

The judges didn't believe Mother's story or mine. I was so hoping that he wasn't coming home. She said to them, if Libby hadn't hit us, then some unknown person must have come into our home. She said the doors in the back were always unlocked, so anybody could have hurt her darling little daughters when the rest of the family were sleeping. She swore on the little flower of Jesus and all the saints she could remember that our wonderful, kind father would never dream of slapping out towards any of his babies.

She told one lie after another to protect him from prison, but the judges could see through her fibs and told her so.

And he was carted off for eighteen months in prison, much to my and Nancy's joy.

That night Nancy and I lay in bed wondering whether he would be hanged or have to face the electric chair or even be shot, as our Keith had us believing that was going to happen to him.

"That would be good," Nancy said. "Then we don't ever have to see the monster again."

A few weeks after Father had been away, Mother told me to get dressed as we were going on a journey together. That's all she would say. I was too scared to ask where we were going.

On the bus, she smoked one Woodbine after another, so I knew she was anxious over something.

We got off the bus at Southall Street, crossed over a main road on the right, and there stood a very old-looking building. I wondered if it was an orphanage, and she was sending me away. It looked a bit similar to the one I had been in when I was Ireland, but this was cold and uninviting.

We were led in through big steel doors and to a courtyard. We were escorted over to a small building by a police guard who smiled kindly at me. Around the structure were iron bars.

Father walked over to Mother and embraced her tenderly, much to my shock and disgust. He cried that he missed her and the 'black stuff' (Guinness). She laughed at him and said she would have a pint for him.

Horrified, I could feel my heart in my chest pounding away. My legs were shaking, and I felt like I was going to faint.

"Well, go to your father then. After all, you little cunt, you put him in here."

I couldn't move. I knew she wouldn't hit me in front of the prison guard, so I said no. Father's and my eyes locked together. I could see the anger and hate he had towards me. I turned away; the feeling was mutual.

Mother told him she only had a half-hour visit with him, and not to waste his time trying to coax me around.

I couldn't believe Mother's loyalty to him. He had raped five of his daughters, and nearly killed two of them. Surely she must see he was the Devil's son, but Mother loved him. He was her life, her everything. Without him, she couldn't function properly.

I was relieved once we were outside the prison walls. I could breathe again. Mother was rabbiting on saying it was our fault that Father raped us. We must have encouraged him in some way or another. I couldn't believe what she was saying. We encouraged him? So my other sisters must have done the same. I didn't quite understand what Mother was talking about, but I got her drift. All his daughters were to blame for the torture and rape he put us through, not him.

With Father away, we didn't see much of Mother, Thankfully. Every few weeks she came home, but would be gone with a blink of an eye. We didn't know where to reach her if there were to be an emergency. We weren't allowed to tell anyone she wasn't with us, on her request.

One day she came home with black eyes, but us kids didn't dare ask her what had happened to her, otherwise we'd end up with black eyes too.

She actually stayed with us for a week, removed her psycho head and put on her caring mother's head like Worzel Gummidge, and looked after the younger siblings. She didn't fool any of us, we were just relieved to have a break from the little ones. My brothers Keith, Martinlee and myself still went out begging for food, but we didn't give Mother any of the money we got. Day after day, we would bring bags of food home. At least we had something to eat if she decided to disappear again.

The rag-and-bone man, Mr McCarthy, was a familiar face around our area, with his big horse called Goliath. Goliath was just beautiful with a big white star on his forehead. His jet-black coat always looked shiny. He was a gentle giant, and all the children adored him.

Mr McCarthy tied Goliath to the lamp post outside the Red Rose pub down our street, something he did every Friday afternoon without fail once he had finished his morning's work. We knew he wouldn't leave the pub till closing time and be as drunk as a lord. His friends would put him on the cart, smack Goliath's arse, and the horse would take his master safely home. For some unknown reason, I believed I could ride a horse because I had ridden a donkey once. Both were the same to me.

Martinlee and Keith jumped up on the cart as I grabbed a hold of the horse's reins, saying "Gee-up," expecting the animal to move. It didn't budge. I kept trying, but the beast was having none of it. He just kept eating whatever was in the food bag that was hanging around his neck. It didn't matter how much the three of us begged him to be a good boy for us, he refused. So Brother Martinlee took it upon himself to jab the pointed end of an old umbrella he found on the cart up the horse's bum. It did the trick.

The beast bolted down the street like a bat out of hell, with the three of us holding on for dear life.

"We're going to die!" cried Martinlee, praying out loud to his favourite saint, Martin de Porres, asking him to please make Goliath stop, and if he couldn't, not to let the Devil take us to Hell, because we were sorry for stealing Mr McCarthy's horse.

The police caught up with us and told us to pull over. Martinlee told them we couldn't because the fucking thing wouldn't stop for us. We were being thrown around like rag dolls.

"You got to shoot it!" Keith screamed.

The traffic had to keep dodging the out-of-control horse. The three of us cuddled together, expecting it to catapult us out of the cart at any second.

After two more circuits around Piccadilly Circus, Goliath suddenly came to a standstill and lifted his tail to relieve his bladder and bowels.

We jumped from the cart as the police came towards us and began running into a Woolworth's store with the police following us. Once we reached the toy department, Keith said we should discard our clothes and put on some costumes to disguise ourselves, so we put on our new outfits and brazenly walked past the store detectives.

We were more or less at the main entrance door to freedom, when the police walked in through the doors.

"You little bastards... that was you on the cart!"

"Sorry, sir, are you talking to us?" I said in my best posh voice.

Mother always said that my voice got on her nerves, because I talk as if I have a plum in my mouth as well as my arse.

"We are fucked," Martinlee said, as we were surrounded by the police and store detectives.

"Looks like we have to fight our way out of this," said Keith.

We stood facing our enemies, dressed in our costumes. Keith, who was Big Chief Sitting Bull, complete with head feathers, raised his plastic tomahawk above his head and threatened to scalp anyone who came near us.

Martinlee, who was dressed as the Lone Ranger, drew his two silver revolvers to shoot the police.

I was dressed as the Lone Ranger's sidekick Tonto. I put an arrow in my bow, ready to take aim.

One police officer said he had had enough of us clowning around, but we weren't, we were deadly serious.

One store detective took a step towards our Martinlee to grab his arm. I let go of my arrow, catching a chancing blow by his right eye.

He howled, "You little cow!"

I couldn't believe I'd hit my target, considering I could only see out of one eye; the other was covered with a pink patch because I had a great big stye on my eye, and the doctor had had to open it and drain it. He'd given Mother antibiotic ointment to prevent reoccurrence, and I had to wear the stupid patch until it was completely better.

We were stripped of our weapons, frogmarched out of the store and taken to the police station.

Once there, we were put into a little room and told not to move. A few policemen's coats were hanging up in the room. Going through the pockets, Martinlee found a big bar of chocolate. We were sat eating it when the sergeant came in.

"That looks nice," he said. "Where did you get it?"

"It's ours," I replied.

"We didn't steal it," laughed Keith.

Martinlee kicked him in the foot to shut him up.

The sergeant looked at us suspiciously as he put his hand into his coat pocket. "You little bastard! You stole that from me."

"Firstly, we are not bastards, we got a mother and father. Maybe not good ones, but we got them. Secondly, you lot may have arrested us a half-a-dozen times in as many months, but no charge was brought against us, so now you are trying to frame us," said Keith. "Thirdly… we found the chocolate on your floor. It's not our fault if you didn't put it in your pocket properly, is it?"

The cell door opened, and another officer entered. He was told to escort us to a larger waiting room where we were given fish and chips and some water to drink.

We were kept in the room until the next morning, when the police had found out who we were and where we lived. We wouldn't give our identities or our address, hoping that if they couldn't find our family, we would have to be put in a children's home. Unlucky for us, one of the police officers, who had been off-duty when we were brought in, recognised us and we were taken back to Mother, who wasn't very pleased to see us or the police.

Woolworth's allowed us to keep our stolen outfits because Mother and Father were threatening to sue them, saying they hadn't handed us back our own clothes, which were nearly new. Of course, the head officer hadn't seen the rags that we'd left behind in the store. If they did, they would have laughed at Mother's threat.

The store detective also dropped his complaint of assault. I think the bosses at his store told him to, but he said he'd dropped them because I hadn't deliberately aimed the bow and arrow at him. Obviously I had.

Goliath the horse was no worse the wear for his adventure with us. Mr McCarthy hadn't even noticed he had gone.

Mother's Gone Again

Mother decided to do one of her disappearing acts once again. She just got up from bed, got dressed, and left without saying anything. Since Father was put away, our gas and electric were cut off because she didn't pay any bills; we had no hot water in the taps, they didn't care. They happily drank any money themselves.

Her days away turned into weeks. We began feeling a bit afraid. What if she never came back? I think we knew somehow she wouldn't, but we hoped she would. After all, surely she would worry about what was happening with the little ones. But the babies didn't seem to be bothered who cared for them, as long as one of us fed them and gave them cuddles.

Keith said: "What if the Welfare people get to know that Mother has abandoned us?"

"They won't," brother Martinlee said. "We'll just carry on as if she's here."

Mother couldn't take responsibility for anything without Father. She needed him to take control of everything. She knew she couldn't boss us around anymore without Father there. She must have realised she had no control over her kids like Father did, but only because we feared him and not her.

Aunt Matilda wasn't our real auntie, but we called her that anyway out of respect for her. In our gypsy culture, we called everyone Auntie or Uncle. It is something of a law amongst our community still to this day. She told us she'd received a letter from our mother, saying she was in a place called Chatham, Kent. We wondered who wrote the letter for Mother, as she couldn't read or write.

Mother said she was suffering from something called post-natal depression after the loss of her twin baby girls. A doctor had given her pills to help her cope. Once she was well enough, she would return to us, so we'd got to be good and look after the babies until then.

Aunt Matilda told us not to mention Mother's absence because the money she was getting would stop, and if that happened, she wouldn't be able to come home with presents for all of us.

"What a load of shit!" Keith said. "Since when did Mother buy presents?"

"Keep your mouth shut, Keith, if you don't want to be separated from this lot," said Auntie Matilda.

Once she had gone, I asked Martinlee what post-natal depression was.

"I think it's something to do with the postman. It was his fault Mother did a bunk on us."

"What did he do so wrong for her to run away from him?" I asked.

"I believe he didn't deliver Father's letter from the prison to her."

"You mean, he kept her letter for pure spite?" I said. "Why?"

"Don't know, but he did look a bit dodgy to me," said Keith.

"I guess so."

"So where did she lose the girls?" asked Nancy.

"She must have been looking after someone else's kids. Probably got drunk and forgot where she left them… like she did once with Sam and didn't know she had lost him until the landlord from the Red Rose pub brought him back to us," said brother Martinlee.

Our water supply had been cut off for over a month now.

"Why is a man with a big fat head down our water drain outside our house?" Nancy asked as she stared out of the window, sticking her tongue out at him.

"I don't know. Maybe he's putting the water back on," I said, opening the door. "Hi, mister. What are you doing?"

"Just making sure no one has been tampering with it," he replied.

"Can you put the water back on for us?" Nancy asked.

"Of course not! Your parents have to pay the bill first."

Our Nancy began crying at that stage, I cuddled her and cried with her. Any emotions we had left were all over the place. It was bad enough being abandoned by all; now we were completely fucked. We just kept lying to all the neighbours and making excuses about where our mother was.

"Don't get upset, sis," Keith said, putting his arms around me. "Remember, you are the sidekick, Tonto. You can't give up on us. What will happen to the family if you do that? Anyway, we're better off than most of the feckers living on the street. We have the range fire burning day and night for the babies when some only have one burning in the evening."

Yes, he was right, but what about once the old furniture in the house had all gone? And I knew Mother would kill us for burning it. *Can't be worrying over that now,* I thought.

Brother Martinlee came up with a great plan. The old man next door to us didn't have a backyard gate to his property, so it would be very easy for one of us to sneak into his yard and use his water tap without him knowing.

Twice a day, one of my brothers, Martinlee or Keith, and I would fetch water in an old tin bucket.

I pulled Father's and Mother's mattress into the front room and the boys' two piss-stained ones from their bedroom upstairs. I figured if we all slept in the same room, we could save a lot of our candles by just using two rooms in the house instead of the whole property. Plus, Keith was frightened that somehow Sergeant Brady would escape from prison and find out that our mother had left us alone and try to steal one of us like he had with brother Keith.

"At least we would feel a bit safer at night," he continued to say.

Brother Martinlee suggested we had to be extra careful to double-check the back door and the front windows to be sure that everything was well locked up properly before we went to bed, plus when we were all out stealing. We knew we had to be very vigilant so that none of us got caught, just in case we bumped into Brady again. We did ask some of the gavers (police) whether they had seen him and to let us know when he was back on duty again. The officers told us to get lost, and if they saw us roaming the streets again, we would be nicked.

I told Martinlee that Keith was freaking me out with all his tales about the nutter who tried to kidnap him. I was sick of telling him that Brady was probably locked up for killing those lads.

"Surely, he wouldn't be walking the streets of Manchester."

"I wouldn't have thought so," Martinlee replied.

I can't say I took to playing mother and father to my young siblings gracefully. They were demanding on me some days and left my brain screaming inside my skull. Some days I would go out on my own begging and leave my brothers home to do the caring of them. I just needed a break from their crying and having to scrub Father's old shirts in cold water that I used for nappies. The constant attention I had to give them always dragged me down. Stealing food to feed them was the easy part. Looking after four of them, all under five-years-old, was quite daunting, plus there was still Nancy, Martinlee, Keith, and myself to worry over.

"Jesus!" I cried one night. "I am only nine years old! You can't expect me to do all this stuff. I'm going to the Welfare to ask for some help," I told Keith.

"You can't do that, Bridie. We all will be taken away to different homes. We got to stay together until Mother gets home."

Things were getting so bad, I couldn't help screaming at the little ones to stop whining for food. Martinlee and Keith were doing their best to keep the others' hungry bellies full. Some days my brothers and I didn't eat because we knew there wouldn't be enough to go around all of us. I would do my best to make money last as long as possible. We'd go out begging to buy candles, coals for the fire, bread, milk, and a lollipop each for the little ones.

Martinlee would kill a couple of pigeons for me with his catapult, and I would boil them up. Once cooked, we'd share them amongst ourselves. There wasn't a lot of meat on them, but at least it was some kind of food to eat. My brothers began going into rubbish bins behind the restaurants and cafés in Piccadilly Centre for any food the businesses threw away. To them, it was just waste – to us, it was life itself. A lot of the food would be all mixed up with cabbage, bits of apple pies, bits of fish and meat, and all different flavours of ice cream that had melted. I have to say it tasted delicious to us. Food was food, no matter what it looked like or where it came from.

Sometimes, Martinlee and Keith would be dragged out of the big bins and told if they returned that the police would be called on them. I couldn't understand why us taking dirty food would be a problem for anyone. It was going to be dumped anyway.

We stopped going to the bins in the end. We didn't need the police coming around and knowing that we'd been abandoned for three months now. The fear of us being found out was tremendous. I knew I had bad days with the children, but I would rather us starve to death than be separated from them. We tried our best to avoid unwanted attention from anyone. Sometimes it was hard not to. We didn't know how long we could carry on, but Martinlee, Keith and I had given up wishing our older sisters would come back to rescue us. They didn't know we had been left on our own, but in reality, they had left us without a care anyways. My heart hardened to them. As far as I was concerned, they didn't bother to check at any time to see how their young siblings were doing. I'll never understand why.

I began telling people's fortunes to make money. I don't know if I was good or not, but people were quite happy to give me the sixpence I asked for.

On the street, if the folks looked rich, I would ask for sixpence. More often than not, I was only given tuppence, but it was better than nothing. It amazed me how people hungered to know their future, whilst I hungered for food. I was surprised by how some adults were willing to tell me all their woes. To be honest, I didn't really listen to them, I just kept nodding my head in agreement. I don't know how they expected a nine-year-old child to advise them what to do about their problems, but they did. One man asked me whether he was going to win the football pools. I had no idea what he was talking about, so I said no. He took back his penny that he had given me. My sister Nancy called him a fat pig and hoped he would break a leg for being so spiteful to us.

A few weeks later, we saw him in Piccadilly with two crutches and a plaster cast on his right leg. We couldn't stop giggling. We must have jinxed the old cunt!

Queenie, Father's fancy woman as Mother would call her, spotted us. She came over to ask us about him. I said the prison had shot him and then hung him to make sure he was dead.

She looked at us strangely and walked away. Of course, I knew Father wasn't killed; it was just wishful thinking on my part. I was quite angry that anyone would want to know about his well-being after what he'd done.

Once home, I told Keith about bumping into Queenie. He said I had to understand that she only knew what the local newspaper had written. The whole truth was kept hidden from them and the court because the doctors in the hospital didn't examine us properly. They let us down in more ways than one. Once Nancy and I were well enough, we were sent home to our parents without any follow-ups. Maybe if they had, my brothers and sisters wouldn't have been in the situation we found ourselves in now.

We were living like animals. Keith and Martinlee would continue to ask the butcher down the road for bones for our imaginary dog. I'm sure by now the butcher had realized we didn't actually have a dog but still handed over the bones regardless. There wasn't enough meat on the bones to keep a dog alive, let alone nine starving kids. I boiled them; once cooked and left to go cold we all chewed on them as if it was a three-course meal we were eating. My two younger siblings had to make do with bread and milk. Martinlee got bread from old Mr Gardener's dustbin, who lived four doors away from us. Mr Gardener asked Martinlee what the fuck he was doing in his bin. Martinlee replied that he was looking for scraps to feed the birds in Alexandra Park. It took us ages to cut off the green mould on the bread before we could give it to the babies.

I wished that Mrs Mullen was still living across the road from us. She had moved away after Father attacked me and my sister Nancy. I got up one morning and saw all her nice furniture being loaded onto vans. I ran across to her house to see what was happening. She explained that she hadn't been well for some time and was moving to Liverpool to be near her sister. She gave me Amy's teddy bear, the one with the floppy ears, and asked me to look after it for her until she saw me again. I couldn't believe she was moving away. She didn't look sick to me. I was heartbroken; she was going away. It seemed to me that everyone I loved would either die on me or move away. I was grateful to her that she trusted me to look after her dead daughter's teddy, but unfortunately, we never did meet up again. I often wondered if she ever thought about me like I did her. Every time I looked at Floppy, I remembered the kind lady with the gentle heart who had loved me for me… nits and all.

Mother saw me crying that morning and said: "I hope you're not whingeing over that old cunt moving. It's her fault your father is doing eighteen months in prison for putting her nose into somebody else's business like ours."

I wanted to say if it wasn't for Mrs Mullen calling the police that night, myself and Nancy would have been killed. Thank God she'd heard our screams. Other neighbours must have, but chose to ignore them. I didn't say anything back to Mother – I didn't fancy having my ears boxed again.

1963

The year was 1963. Months had gone by, and still no sign of Mother. We didn't know how much longer we could continue living like feral children. The little ones stank like skunks, in spite of us doing our best to keep them clean. We had run out of torn-up shirts because we didn't have enough water to wash them, so used old jumpers that belonged to Mother to put on the babies' arses. Their little bums were badly blistered, and every time they had a wee, they'd scream with pain. I couldn't take them to a clinic to get some cream for their bottoms in case they asked questions. The last thing we wanted was for them to know that Mother and our older brothers and sisters had abandoned us, walked away, and forgotten about us. I wondered if we would ever see any of them again – or if I wanted to, for that matter.

Wednesday started off as a normal day for us. Martinlee and Keith were going out for the day, stealing food and begging. Mine and Nancy's job was to look after the other kids and try to clean up the pigsty rooms that we all slept and ate in.

After months of keeping the window shutters safely locked, I decided to open them up to let some fresh air come into the rooms. It was the first time that natural light was allowed in since Mother left us. I persuaded myself opening the shutters was a good idea after living in darkness for so long and the only light we had was from candles that we burned day and night. Once everyone was in bed, then and only then were they blown out. If we couldn't steal them, we'd get them from some of the neighbours, saying, "Mother said, could she borrow a few candles until she gets her Welfare money to put our electric on?" They always obliged us with some.

Fifteen-month-old Steven and nine-month-old Paul turned their little faces away from the light that was coming in through the window. I thought I had blinded them because they kept squinting their eyes. They hadn't seen daylight since we were left on our own. I didn't see the point in taking them out begging with me in the cold weather. What if the police or store detectives gave chase after me? It would be very unlikely I could get away running with four kids in a big pram. Best they stay indoors where they would be safe.

Looking back, it was a very foolish thing to do, but I was only nine years old and having to be mother and father to my siblings. I'd been shoved into an adult role, instead of being just one of the children. I was terrified that some bad person would break into the ugly house and steal one of them, or maybe all of them. Keith's lucky escape was always at the forefront of my mind. I didn't know if the same people would come after the rest of us. Trying to keep them safe was my top priority, and if it meant that I had to keep them inside the house with shutters on the windows shut, so be it.

Once my brothers returned home with their stolen goodies of sausages and potatoes, I set about cooking the evening meal, or should I say burning it. We all settled down for the night. The house was at peace; only the sound of the babies breathing could be heard.

I whispered to Keith that I had an awful feeling in my stomach, as if something bad was going to happen.

"Like what?" he said.

"I don't know."

"Go to sleep; everything will be okay. You'll see."

I drifted off into a very restless sleep…

Banging. Was I dreaming that someone was trying to get into our home?

The banging got louder and louder. Father's voice yelling in the letterbox, "Open the fucking door!"

By now, all the kids were awake – we were shitting ourselves.

"Jesus, Keith! I thought the prison people had killed him!" Nancy cried.

"So did I," replied Keith.

"What are we going to do?" asked Martinlee.

"Maybe it's not him, just his ghost," Nancy cried.

"I thought ghosties went BOOO," whispered Keith. "Shush! If we keep quiet, he may go away."

The banging didn't stop. We could hear Father's voice yelling, "Open this door now, you little cunts."

He knew we were in because baby Paul started crying and took to one of his fits of screaming.

"What took you so fucking long to open the fucking door to me?" he yelled at me.

"I didn't hear you, I just woke up," I said, lying.

The red streetlights next to our front door made his face glow bright red. He had put on a lot of weight since I last saw him.

"Where's your fucking no good bitch of a mother?"

"I don't know," I said in a shaky voice.

"I see there is no fucking electric," he said.

A voice in my head was telling me to run. *Look,* it was saying, *the front door is wide open. You can run past him. He's too pissed to catch you.* But I knew I couldn't run anywhere without the little ones, especially my sister Nancy.

I couldn't think straight with fear running through my body. I was in sheer panic as to what to do next.

"I am going out looking for your cunt of a mother. When I find her, I'll fucking killing her for not fucking bothering to come and see me. Not even a letter from the fucking dirty cow. Make sure you and Nancy are in my bloody bed waiting for me when I get back. Do you fucking hear me?"

"Yes, Daddy," I replied.

I would have said anything just to get him out of the house, but I knew there was no way he was going to put his grubby hands on me or our Nancy again, or putting his grubby Willy Wonka in our mouths again, no way I was swallowing his disgusting smelly urine, not again. *I'd rather die*, I thought.

Before he left the house, he grabbed me by my throat, squeezing so tight. I could see the hate and discontent in his mad eyes that he had for me.

"Open the fucking door the next time you hear me calling. Do you hear me?"

I couldn't answer him as I was gagging for my breath. He walked out the door looking at me and said he'd be back soon.

I told my brothers Martinlee and Keith to make up some bottles for the four babies because we were all getting out of this house before he got back. We didn't have time to wait for the water to boil – they would have to have cold powdered milk.

I said, "The Devil could be back at any minute, hurry up."

Nancy and I set about getting the little ones dressed as Keith and Martinlee carried the big old pram out onto the street. We had no idea where we were going, but anywhere was better than here right now.

Once we got to the top of our street, Keith and I returned to the ugly house to burn it down. We didn't think about our next-door neighbours each side of our house or about their homes burning down as well. At that moment, our concern was that if the police found us on the streets, they wouldn't be able to take us back to a burnt house.

We set light to a load of old clothes in Father's bedroom and did the same to all the other bedrooms upstairs. We watched the flames take their toll. All the pain and humiliation he'd put his children through, I hoped it would all burn away with the ugly house.

Martinlee was becoming increasingly nervous. He was expecting Father to come around the corner at any moment. He was clutching his old medal; I had got it for him as a Christmas present. He was praying to God to help us.

It was a great feeling that we would never have to go back to that house again.

It was two o'clock in the morning when the police found us walking the cold streets of Manchester. They bundled us all into a black van, pram and all. For once, the police were a welcome sight to us.

Once we got to the police station, a policewoman made us some egg sandwiches. Eating them was like we had gone to Heaven and back. The youngsters were given warm milk and sucked the bottles dry. There was no need to ask for our names or address as one of the police officers remembered brothers Martinlee and Keith and me when we had stolen the outfits from the Woolworth's store: he had arrested us.

With a grin on his face, he asked were we still using the names we'd used when he first arrested us.

"Why would we when you know our real names?" Martinlee said.

A place was found for all of us for the night in a local children's home called Broom House. It was too late for us to take a bath. We all slept in the same room on a large mattress, as we refused to go in separate rooms.

After a breakfast of hot tea, cornflakes, and lots of slices of bread and jam, the police van returned to take us to another home that had lots of room for us; it was called Nazareth House in Preston, Manchester, and was run by nuns.

Three very old nuns met us at the door.

As the police waved goodbye, one of them said to me: "We won't be seeing you little feckers for some time."

How wrong was he?

The van drove away. Martinlee and Keith took to their heels and disappeared fast down the long drive, leaving me screaming after them to come back. They stopped at the end of the drive and yelled at me to run, but I couldn't because of the youngsters who were already upset with the commotion going on around them and seeing strange faces they didn't know.

My best friends had gone out of sight and out of my life: *Just swallow me now world,* I thought. *Oh no, second thoughts, spit me back out world, I need to look after the babies.*

The next time I would see them again, they would be married with children of their own: now Keith was seven, Martinlee was eight. They shouted their echoing goodbyes while running through the street.

I felt desperately tired and, at the same time, a sense of relief, knowing Father couldn't get his hands on us again.

The nuns bathed us all, washed our hair, and dressed us in new clean clothes. White ointment was put on the babies' bums to help them heal.

Nazareth House was home for me and my five siblings for three years. During that time, Mother never came to visit us, much to our relief. The nuns were good to us and tried very hard to understand me. They did their best to make all the seventy-odd children in the home happy, but my sister Nancy and I were very withdrawn and would always recoil from the slightest suggestion of a hug. We spent a lot of time crying for Keith and Martinlee, as they were not only our brothers but our best friends. We trusted no one, and although the home was full of kids, we felt lonely and isolated. The four babies no longer needed us because the nuns took care of their every need.

After being in the home for three months, Mother Kelly arranged for me to go to a nearby girls' school, praying that I would make friends, but instead, I made enemies. I seemed to be at war with the whole world and fought with anyone who tried to befriend me.

My form teacher and I took an instant dislike to one another. Mrs Greenway was a large woman – she had to walk into the classroom sideways. The first thing that greeted you was her gigantic belly. It seemed to hang down over her knees. She didn't have a normal chair to sit on – she had a bench. I had never seen a pair of hairy legs like hers. The black hair on them was so long you could have plaited it. She was in her early forties, and the rumour was that when her husband left her, he left a note saying he had paid the milkman's bill… it was the milkman he had run off with.

One day she wrote something on the blackboard and asked me to read it to the class. I didn't have a clue what it said and told her so. The old witch knew I couldn't read, and now the whole class knew as well. I felt utterly humiliated. It didn't take long before word got around that Dumbo, as she called me, lived at an orphanage, and some girls kept asking why my parents had sent me away. I told them my mother and father had been killed in a car crash. I lied – but the lie took the wind out of their sails and they stopped questioning me.

I became very aggressive. I suppose you could say I found my voice and my fists against the bullies. The slightest bad comment towards me from one of them and I would lash out. I didn't have my brothers to fight my battles anymore, so I had to protect myself.

I was very angry towards the male teachers and refused point-blank to attend their classes, plus the poor fathers of other pupils had to bear my insults at them.

It was decided by the school headmistress that I shouldn't attend the school any longer. St Mary's had had enough of me and I'd had enough of them. I would be schooled at the orphanage.

Mother Jude bundled me into the small study room one day, saying the psychiatrist doctor had come to see me.

"Why?" I asked. "I ain't sick."

"We let him be the judge of that, shall we?" she replied, closing the door behind her. The doctor sat with his back to the door.

"Come and sit down, my child," he said.

My intention was to run, but the door wouldn't open. Why would Sister Jude lock it, knowing I had a fear of closed doors? They didn't know why, as I didn't give any explanation. All the nuns knew about my family was our names and that we had been found walking the streets in the pouring rain.

The doctor stood up. He was tall and thin and wore a navy-blue suit and gold-rimmed glasses. Fear welled up in me as he said again to come, sit down, holding out his hands to me. A tornado of emotions – fear, fury, panic – whirled up from the depths of my being as he came towards me. My heart was pumping so fast as I felt trapped. Visions of my father locking me in rooms before he raped me spun around my brain like a whirlwind. I had to get out of the room before he attacked me, not that the poor man had any intention of doing that, but I wasn't to know he was there just to talk to me until after the event. With trembling legs, I ran at him, clawing at his face and knocking his glasses off. I grabbed one of the little wooden stools and threw it at the window which shattered into pieces. I was ready to jump from the four-storey building, not thinking I could be seriously hurt, or worse, die.

Several nuns ran into the room. Two grabbed me away from the window. Others dealt with the white-faced, shaking doctor. The psychiatrist was given a glass of medicinal brandy before he sped away down the drive in his shiny red car. I never met him again.

Paddy Smith

One cold, frosty morning, a new boy arrived at the home. You could hear his screaming and shouting all over the building. His name was Paddy Smith, and he was twelve years old.

He had carrot-red hair, which stood on end as if he had seen a ghost, and the most freckled face I had ever seen. It was love at first sight for me. For the next year, we were inseparable, and I never fought with him as I had with some of the other boys. Life was worth living again.

Although Paddy Smith was short, plump, and very ugly, I adored him. We had so much in common it was unbelievable. His mum had twenty-two kids, same as mine; he hated his father like I did; he disliked fish and ice cream, plus we enjoyed the same sort of pranks, and I would fiercely defend him against anyone who picked on him.

We all had to help with the chores at the home. It was our turn to make the beds, so we made them apple-pie-style, by turning the top sheet back on itself and filling the beds with scrubbing brushes and marbles and toothpaste. The best bit was hiding in the alcove on the staircase to peep round the dormitory door and watch the kids' reactions when they jumped into bed and landed on a scrubbing brush.

My favourite job was polishing the wooden parquet floors in the corridors and halls. An Indian girl called Maria Smith used to help me. We had special pads strapped on, so we did not get sore knees. There was a huge tin of lavender wax polish in the cleaning cupboard and boxes of yellow dust cloths for us to do the job. It gave me a great sense of satisfaction to see the wooden floor gleaming like glass.

But my true motivation behind doing the work were my moments of glory when I tied the dusters to my feet and skated down the long corridors and around the hall, watching myself in the big mirrors and pretending to be a world-famous ballerina. That was my burning ambition for a long time, but I didn't share my dream with the nuns, only Maria. She was a coloured girl the same age as me, and she had the same desire as me. She brought back ballet books from her school library for me. The colourful pictures of the costumes that the women wore were out of this world. I could see myself walking on stage with the most famous dancers ever, like Margot Fonteyn. My name was in lights alongside theirs at the Royal Festival Ballet, the audience throwing red and yellow roses on the stage as I danced, followed of course by tumultuous applause, several curtain calls and cascades of fresh, beautiful flowers at my feet. The ugly duckling was now transformed into something gorgeous. Well, in my mind, anyway.

One morning after prayers and telling God I was so sorry for my sins, Sister Mary Joseph told us that the Round Table organisation had offered to pay for and organise a holiday to Wales for twelve children from the home. I couldn't believe my luck when I was one of the children chosen to go but was worried about leaving my brothers and sisters behind, as this would be the first time I had been away from them. I also expressed my feelings that I would miss Paddy Smith. I was quite upset that he wasn't allowed to go with us. Sister Ann-Maria assured me that my siblings and Paddy would be taken great care of – a bit of time away from them wouldn't do any harm to them or me.

Our holiday day arrived. I was sorry to say goodbye to my family and Paddy Smith. He was one of my best friends: him and Maria Smith were the only people I felt close to since the departure of my brothers Martinlee and Keith. I suppose he took the place of all the people I had lost along the way of my life.

The holiday was fantastic. I couldn't believe that here I was, running on a beach that seemed to go on for miles, without a care in the world.

We were staying in a large house with a gigantic back garden. Seating benches were scattered all around the grounds, and a large fishpond that looked to be overflowing with fish of all colours and sizes took my breath away. I had never seen anything like them.

Rhos-on-Sea in Wales was the most beautiful place on earth to me, apart from Ireland.

The day before we were due to return home to the convent, we were given pocket money. I stared in amazement when Sister Joseph handed me £3. I couldn't understand why she was giving it to me. I hadn't begged or told her fortune for it. Maybe she was just testing me in some way or other, I thought.

I tried to hand it back, but she refused saying, "Don't buy too many sweets, now, with my gift money."

I bought all my brother's and sister's little bags of chocolate buttons. For Paddy, I got him a Sindy doll. I knew he would be in his element with my present to him. I hid it from the nuns because they believed that boys should play with boys' toys and girls with girls'. He would sneak into my room every night to dress and put the doll's hair into plaits. He loved Susan Redstone's paper doll, which had lots of different garments to mix and match. I had to admit he did look quite cute when he dressed up in our clothes. All this was kept secret from the nuns until Sister Mary found him asleep cuddling a doll one of the girls had given him as a birthday present. She was not amused and demanded to know who he had stolen it from.

Poor Smithy, that was the nickname the girls gave him. His punishment was to spend the night in the home's chapel and beg God's forgiveness. It didn't bother him about spending the night in the church, but it was heart-breaking that she took his doll away from him.

I noticed a few days back from holiday that the nuns split Paddy and me at mealtimes. He asked Sister Joseph what we had done wrong and was told he was a bad influence on the other boys in the home. She didn't go into the full details with him, but he was very upset that he wasn't allowed to go near or play with the young boys again. The nuns made him out to be some kind of monster because he liked playing with dollies. I didn't see anything bad about that. After all, I played football with some of the lads.

Two years to the day he came to Nazareth House, his parents arrived to take him home. He refused to go to them. His father grabbed his arm, and Paddy kicked out at him as he physically carried Smithy down the stairs and into a waiting taxi.

Then he was gone, out of my life forever.

Once again, I was alone. I cried for months over the loss of my best friend and had many screaming tantrums with the nuns. How they put up with me, only their God knows.

A few months after Smithy's departure, I received a letter from my mother. I couldn't read, so Sister Rose read it for me, stating that she was coming to take us to our new home in Kent. There was no information on her whereabouts for the last three years and whether she was with our abusive father.

Such confusion arose in me. I did not want to go. After years in Nazareth House, it felt like home to me and my brothers and sisters. There was safety and warmth and security here.

The letter said she was coming to fetch us all in two weeks' time. I did my best not to show my anxiety to my younger siblings, who by now couldn't remember their parents and had no recollection of the past. Lucky for them. As for myself and my sister Nancy, we were still bearing the scars from what had happened to us, and probably will for the rest of our lives.

Sunday, the day before Mother was due to pick us up, we got dressed in our best clothes to go to church. I took stock of what I would be leaving behind. I just loved the little frilly Sunday dresses, the straw boaters with blue ribbons, and my neat white socks and shiny black buttoned shoes. I looked around the dormitory of four little beds with plain matching white bedspreads and the four highly polished bedside lockers where we kept our few personal belongings. I would miss some of the kindly nuns bustling and fussing around us all day. They were always working – scrubbing, cleaning, washing, and pressing our clothes and praying – I never saw them idle.

Next morning found me and my five young brothers and sisters all clean and tidy, waiting in the entrance hall for Mother to arrive. A taxi pulled up at the door, and there she was. Her beautiful long black hair was replaced with shoulder-length, auburn-coloured hair. She wore a white blouse, black pencil skirt, and black stiletto-heeled shoes. She looked very glamorous, and when she spoke, it was in her posh voice.

The nuns helped us all to climb into the taxi, the young ones protesting noisily at the prospect of leaving their home with a virtual stranger.

The doors slammed, and the nuns waved goodbye as we were driven away down the long gravel drive.

Moving South

Once we got to the end of the drive, the taxi pulled over, and Father got in. I felt as though the world was turning upside down, like a baby bird tipped out of its nest before it was ready to fly. How could Mother still be with him?

She seemed to know what I was thinking and said, "It will be okay now. Your father will never hurt ya again. He promised... Didn't you?" she said to him.

He nodded his head in agreement with her without taking his eyes off me.

We followed Father and Mother silently into the train bound from London. We must have looked a bewildered little bunch: the four younger children hanging onto myself and Nancy, as though we were the only familiar sight on an alien landscape. They viewed Father and Mother with deep scepticism. After all, they were virtual strangers to them.

Another train from London took us to Chatham in Kent. Our new home was in Hill Street. It was a neat-and-tidy-looking house; four bedrooms, no bathroom, a small front room, a kitchen, and an outside toilet. The back garden was nice with all different coloured flowers growing in it. The other side had a big fence and a gate to keep Father's chickens that he sold to restaurants and Indian takeaways. He would buy two or three dozen every week to sell on. Nancy and I would have to sit in the garden for hours, plucking and gutting the smelly chickens. How we hated it.

One day, Mother introduced us to our next-door neighbour. Mr Johnson had the most pointed-looking head we had ever seen on a human being. Mother told us later on his poor mother must have had forceps when he was born. We had no idea what she was talking about. I asked her what had that got to do with his funny-shaped head.

"Forceps are metal salad tongs used to help him get out."

"Out of what?" I asked.

"Her fucking arse!"

The thought of him coming out of his mum's arse made me feel sick. He must have been six feet tall and very fat. *No wonder his poor mum had had trouble to get him out of her bum,* I thought.

I was thirteen years old and had no idea where babies came from or how to get one. There was no point asking Mother as she was a Catholic and believed it was forbidden to tell me, so one day, Nancy and I got the courage to ask Mr Johnson with the pointed head.

His bulging eyes stared at us for a few seconds before he replied: "Can't you ask your mother?"

"Mother said to ask you because you are full of wisdom," I said.

I think he knew I was lying, but went ahead anyway and told us about the big white stork who fished us out from the water and delivered us to our lucky parents in the dead of night and popped us through an open window.

"See your birthmark on your face?" he said to me. "Well, the stork's bill bit into your face during transit."

"God, you must have been a heavy baby to carry!"

"The stork couldn't have got me from the sea because I cannot swim," Nancy told him.

"Well, it got you from under a gooseberry bush then. Where were you born?" he asked Nancy.

"England."

"Well, he got you from the lovely gardens of England."

"I'm from Ireland," I said boldly.

"Then, you were fished out of the beautiful Irish Sea."

We were so chuffed to hear that we had come from very special places, not out of Mother's arse.

For some weeks, life was good for us. Our parents were really trying to make a 'go' of family life. Mother did her best to keep the housework under control, and Father was managing to stay clear of drink, and kept well away from Nancy and me. But within weeks, tension began to mount on the home front once again. They spent more and more time at the pub, and when they came home, the arguments followed. When Father was drunk, Nancy and I shook with fear.

One afternoon Father was in his usual alcoholic state. There was a sharp rap at the back door. It was the DHSS man. He was a nervous little man, twisting his cap in his hands.

"Father, someone to see you," I called.

Father staggered out into the garden with a pan of hot tomato soup in his hands. The DHSS man backed away from him a few steps down the garden path.

"Sir, you're drunk," he said, in answer to my father's barrage of abuse. He clutched his clipboard tighter, twisted his cap a bit more, and then repeated, "Sir, you're very drunk! I cannot talk to you in that state."

"You've said that once too often!" yelled my father, lunging at him with the saucepan and smothering his neatly-pressed grey suit with tomato soup.

The poor man hurried for the gate to get away from Father, but before he could reach it safely, our Jack Russell dog called Lany had him by the trouser leg and was trying to pull him back into the house. Eventually, he escaped and ran full pelt down the road away from the nutty house, with his turn-ups flapping in shreds.

Father did not receive any Social Security money for a fortnight after that.

Father was quite insistent that we children should regularly attend the Catholic Church. They were very good at keeping an eye on needy families and helping out with food, clothes and money to pay the bills. It wasn't that he believed in God, but the money the priest gave us to give to him kept him going with a drink.

I hated going to Mass. The service was in Latin and very formal. Stand up, sit down: I could not understand why we had to go through all that ritual to find God. I remember Sister Margaret in Ireland saying that God loved me and could hear my prayers even when I whispered them into my pillow.

There was no way to avoid the service as Father always checked up on us by asking us what colour robes the priest was wearing.

One week, I came up with a brilliant plan: I would peep around the church doors and notice the colour of the robes he was wearing, then we could skip off to the park for the morning, away from domestic ties.

We climbed trees, played tag, and got dizzy on the roundabout. I loved the swings. For a few moments, I could soar upwards towards the blue sky, high above the ground, the wind in my hair, and forget all my troubles – fly like a bird! But I always came back to earth with a bump. It was too good to last. The deception worked well for several weeks, but then they began to get suspicious.

"What was Father Keegan wearing today?" asked Father.

"Err, green?"

"No, try again," Father said.

"Oh, yes, that's right," Nancy said, "He was wearing red. I looked in, Bridie didn't."

"So ya didn't go then?"

"Yes, we did, but Bridie wouldn't remember… she fell asleep, didn't you?" Nancy said.

Eventually, she got it right. Father had decided to go to church to check on us. He had become suspicious because we always came home with dirty faces and torn clothes. Father boxed mine and Nancy's ears so hard that our heads rang, and we saw stars.

My Fourteenth Birthday

My fourteenth birthday came and went without anyone giving a damn. I was singing 'Happy Birthday' all day, hoping my parents would take the hint. They didn't. It was just another day for them.

Mr Johnson found me in our garden the next morning crying. In the year I had lived next door to him, we had become good buddies. He had a twenty-year-old daughter who had died of a brain haemorrhage. He showed me a picture of her. She was very pretty. His wife had passed away a year before my family had moved next door to him. He told me he had called the police on my father because he was beating up on my mother before us kids came on the scene. My parents never found out it was him. He disliked my father intensely. As for my mother, he felt sorry for her and couldn't understand why she put up with him and allowed him to hit on her kids.

I looked forward to our morning chats. Once I had got the kids ready for school and had done all the domestic cleaning for Mother, I would go next door to see if Mr Johnson was okay. That was my routine every day. I became my parents' skivvy again. Without having Mr Johnson to talk to, I think I would have died of loneliness.

"What's up with you, girl?" he asked me that morning. I told him about the pain I was in.

"How long have you had the pain, girl?" he said in his deep voice.

He never called me by my name – I didn't really know why and wasn't too bothered about it.

"I got it yesterday."

"Best you tell your mother, girl."

"I did, but she wasn't listening to me."

"Try again," he said.

I did my best to explain to Mother about the pain and cramp I was having in my belly, but all she said was, "What the fuck do you expect me to do about it?"

A bit of sympathy, I thought.

I woke up the next morning, covered in blood.

Terrified that my insides were falling out of my little minny, I didn't know what to do, so I got loads of toilet paper and shoved it down my knickers to hold in my liver and kidneys or whatever was trying to leave my body.

I ran over to Mr Johnson's and banged on his door impatiently. "I'm dying!" I cried as he opened his door to me.

"What's up, girl? Has that pig of a father beat you?"

"No," I said sobbing.

The kind old man listened to all my woes and laughed at me saying, "Oh my girl, no need to worry. You've just become a woman. It happens to all girls. Mind you, you must keep the boys away from you. Don't want another mini-you, do we?"

I didn't have the foggiest idea what he was talking about. What did my periods have to do with boys?

I often wished Mr Johnson was my father. I had no shame in telling him anything or asking his advice on any topic. I have to admit, though, I hated it every month when I had the hormones, the cramps and pain and having no money to pay for sanitary pads. As far as Mother was concerned, they were a waste of money. She gave me two old blouses that were too small for her. I was told to rip them up into pieces and use those instead. The bleeding was another problem for me. Flashbacks would rush back in my brain when Father raped me. So much blood and pain. How I wished I was born a boy.

A few months after my conversation with Mr Johnson, he died in his sleep of cancer. It was said his body was riddled with it. He had taken too many pills for the pain. Some said he committed suicide; others said it was an accidental overdose. Either way, he was dead, and I was devastated. God how I missed him. He was the only friend I had in this lonely life of mine.

Some folks may find it strange that an eighty-four-year-old man would find anything in common with a fourteen-year-old girl. Mainly gardening. His was beautiful. I swear every flower on earth was in his garden, which he tended to lovingly every day. I continued to look after it for the first two weeks after his death until one morning, I was just finishing weeding one of the flower beds when three elderly persons walked in the back gate.

"What are you doing in my brother's property?" asked the woman.

I was a bit taken aback because Mr Johnson never mentioned having a sister and two brothers.

I explained that I was tending Mr Johnson's garden and wished he was here to do it himself because it was hard work without him.

"Well," she said, "You don't need to concern yourself anymore."

"The house is sold, so keep out," said one of the brothers abruptly.

"Now clear off," said the other.

I climbed over the fence to my own home and could feel their beady eyes staring at me.

A few days later, a big white van pulled up outside the old fellow's house. The furniture removal men showed no respect as they carried out the old man's belongings and walked all over the plants and flowers that must have taken Mr Johnson years to plant.

"Get off them, you bald-headed cunt!" I yelled out of my bedroom window at one of them. "You could walk on the path without trampling all over the garden."

"Shut up, you little mongrel," he replied. "What's it got to do with you?"

Nancy collected all the eggs that Father's chickens had laid that morning. We smashed them all over the front of the removal men's van windows. We had a great laugh watching them trying to clean the mess off the van.

They knew it was us but had no proof as we were not seen doing the deed. Father couldn't understand why the chickens hadn't produced any eggs that day.

Nancy and I nodded our heads in agreement with him as if to say we were baffled as well. If he had known what we'd done with his eggs, he would have killed us.

One night, I lay awake, listening to a couple of cats in our garden. It was very dark, all the lights were off, only the street-lamps along the road cast a faint light, and my curtains moving in the breeze were casting shadows on my wall.

There was a shuffling noise outside my door. The handled turned slowly. I heard it squeak. A large shadow crossed the room. The floorboard squeaked. Someone sat on my bed. I could smell alcohol. He or she was pulling the bedclothes off me. I bolted upright in bed, thinking it was Mother who was heavily pregnant with twins and had gone into labour. Once I realised it wasn't her, I let out a loud scream. The shadowy figure left my room. From that moment, I knew I had to get away from there. I knew the danger I was in yet again. Father was back to his old tricks again.

Run, RUN! My head was telling me, but where to? I didn't know anyone to run to.

Not surprisingly, I wasn't going to school; my parents needed me at home, so of course, I had no schoolmates to talk to, and if I did, would I have told them about Father? I doubt it, partly out of embarrassment and fear. I'd probably end up the laughing-stock of the school.

I stole some money from the family home, made my way to Chatham train station, and got the train to Victoria Station. After all, I had heard that the streets in London were paved with gold. Whoever had told that tale was lying.

I walked the roads for hours looking for gold, thinking if I find enough, I'd go back to Manchester, find my three older sisters and beg them to take me in and rescue our Nancy from Father. I had no idea if they were still up North. It had been four years since I'd last seen them. They could be dead for all I knew, but try I must.

My plan sounded brilliant to me, but in reality, it was a no-no from the start. I climbed into a mail carriage and hid behind the mail bags waiting for the train to set off on its journey to Manchester. Unbeknownst to me, two police officers spotted me entering the mail carriage and decided to investigate. Before I knew what was happening, I found myself locked in a tiny little cell in the police station. I refused to give my name or address. I was trying to escape my father – I didn't need these idiots sending me back into his clutches again. A very skinny-looking policewoman brought me in a cup of tea that tasted like dishwater. The cheese sandwich was no better; it was dry and tasted revolting.

"Right," she said. "Let's me and you have a chat. My name's Rita. What's your name?"

I may have only been fourteen years old, but I had a lot more savvy than she gave me credit for.

"Charlene," I said.

"Is that really your name?" she asked.

"Yeah."

"Where do you live?"

"Manchester."

"So, what are you doing in London?"

"Shopping with my two sisters. They must have lost me, and I had to make my way to the railway station, hoping to find them. No luck, so I got on the train to go home. My poor sisters must be devastated by now looking for me. Best you let me go before I miss the midnight train," I said with a smiley grin on my face, thinking I had outsmarted her with my clever answers.

The old battle-axe asked for my address in Manchester. Of course, I gave her my old one, Stamford Street, Hulme, thinking there was no way she could find out I was lying to her.

"What's your surname?"

"Brown."

"So your name is Charlene Brown, and your address is 24 Stamford Street, Hulme, Manchester?" she said.

"Yes," I replied, shoving the dried-up sandwich in my mouth. I hadn't eaten all day, and with the money I had stolen from Father, I had bought a whole new outfit for myself. After all, I needed to look my best if I found my sisters. Didn't want them thinking I was still the scruffy-looking kid they'd left behind in Manchester.

"What are your mum and dad's names?"

"What do you need that information for?" I asked.

"I presume they must be worrying to death, knowing their child is lost somewhere in London."

"I doubt it."

"Why would that be? Don't you get on with them?" asked the policewoman.

"They are both dead."

"Oh dear," she said with a pitiful look on her face. She placed her skinny hands over mine. For a minute, I thought she was going to cry.

"How did your parents pass on?"

"I don't know," I said. "I was only a baby, and my sisters don't talk about what happened. The emotion they suffered was unbearable, hence why I don't push them to find out."

"Did they die separately?" she asked.

"I believe not."

She put her arms around me and asked if I was still hungry.

"A bit," I said through make-believe sobs. "May I have fish and chips, and spotted dick and custard, and if possible a raspberry lollipop? If that's not too much trouble."

"I see what I can do," she replied as she left my cell.

God, I thought, *Mother did say I'd make a good actress.* Mind you; she wouldn't be very happy, me dismissing her and Father as dead. I know some people who would be disgusted with my statement to the police about my parents, but to be honest, I didn't feel like I was lying. To me, it was true, in my mind, at least, especially my father. I didn't give it a second thought about saying what I said. To be tortured and brutally raped time after time, and knowing your mother did nothing about it and made me lie to my aunt Mary Helen just to cover his back was sickening to say the least.

Sergeant Rita returned with my food. It was delicious and tasted even better when she said she'd paid for it out of her own pocket.

She stayed with me for some time, talking to me about her dreams of becoming a copper and what kind of work I would like to do once I left school. I had been in Kent for nine months, and the only part of school I had seen were the gates to pick up my young siblings. As about dreams, the *only* one I had right now was to be on the train to Manchester. I kept my thoughts to myself

She left the cell again, but this time she locked the door. I wanted her to stay with me. I hated being on my own, especially in a room I couldn't escape from. I laid down on the mattress. It felt like I was laying on lead and was so uncomfortable. The cell was so hot. I was hesitating whether to strip down to my knickers and vest, but decided not to. I began to cry. I didn't know why. The cell walls seemed to be moving in on me. The air was stifling. I began to believe I was slowly suffocating. Panic set in. Banging at the cell door, I hoped someone would come to my rescue. My cries for help were completely ignored. Why didn't anyone come? My imagination was running all over the place. What if everyone in the police station had gone home and forgotten I was locked up in the cell?

I felt alone and confused, not for the first time in my short life and probably not the last. My anxiety was hitting me like a ton of bricks. I could hardly move or breathe. *Just ignore it,* I kept telling myself. *It will be all right. You must try and remain relaxed.* Didn't Sister Bernadette used to say 'calmness is the best medicine for the brain' when I would be ranting and raving over something or other? I was willing my mind to concentrate on good things, like meeting my older sisters again. In my mind's eye, I could see them picking me up, swinging me around with delight at our reunion, and all would be well with the world once again. I suppose, in reality, I knew this would never happen. Why would anyone want someone around to remind them of their terrifying past? I didn't blame them for running away from it.

The cell door opened. A policeman and a woman walked in. "This is Mary Day."

I looked her up and down. She was quite a good-looking woman, with green eyes and light blonde hair with blue highlights. She had a red stud in her nose, which I'd never seen before, a long green skirt and a white sleeveless T-shirt.

Wow! I thought, *I love her style!*

"Hello, Bridie," she said.

Fuck! How did she know my name?

"Your parents reported you missing to the police in Kent and will be delighted to know that you've been found," she said.

"Sorry, I think you're mistaking me for someone else," I replied. "My parents are dead… have been for a long time."

"Is this photograph of you?" she handed me the picture.

I looked at it. Sadness pierced my heart. Smiling faces of some of my siblings, myself and Paddy Smith looked back at me. I remembered when the photo had been taken in Nazareth House, the children's home: everything was well with the world, them and me.

Tears filled my eyes as I wondered about Smithy. Was he happy? Did he ever think about the time we spent together in the home? All the crazy things we got up to. Like once we were sent into the convent church to pray to God for forgiveness for dressing Smithy up as a girl. I'd put one of my best Sunday dresses on him with all the frills and bows, my straw hat with the pink ribbons, white knee-length socks, and white sandals. I painted up his face with some of the day helper's makeup. By the time I had finished with him, he looked like something out of a horror movie. We were rolling on the floor with laughter. Sister Maryann was disgusted with us, hence why she dragged both of us by our ears to the church doors and almost pushed us inside the door.

Near the altar was a very large open coffin. Nothing was in it. We both climbed in, Smithy at one end, me at the other. With the quietness and stillness inside the church, we fell asleep in the coffin.

Horrifying screams woke us up. Sitting bolt upright, I could see Sister Bridgette running from the church. Before I knew what was happening, the church was full of a dozen or more nuns. Sister Jennifer, with the glass eye, called us evil children. Her sidekick Sister Catherine said God would never forgive us for showing disrespect to Mother Mary's resting bed. Mother Mary was the head of the home, though we had never met her. She was the one who decided what punishment, if any, we would receive for our bad behaviour.

"Does that mean, now she has passed away, you got no authority to lay any kind of punishment on us?" asked Smithy.

A slap across Smithy's face gave us the answer.

Mother Mary was placed in her coffin the next day, dressed in her white and black habit. A crown of red roses was placed around her head, a cross laid across her chest, and rosary beads in her hand. She was quite old and very tall. I can't say seeing a dead person disturbed me that much. After all, didn't I see my brother Paul Roy when he had passed?

The service seemed to go on for hours. Father Doyle was very old with a stutter, and he stuttered every other word. No wonder the Mass was taking so long. I swear he fell asleep standing near the altar. Now and then, he would shake his head, as if to bring himself around, and say, "Where was I?"

Maureen Brittson, who was a Protestant and who had only been in the home a few weeks, asked me why all the services were in Latin.

"I think all the priests come from Latin."

"You reckon?"

"Yes."

"How far is Latin from Manchester?" she asked.

Smithy said it was God's language, so it must be in a holy country, somewhere like Canterbury in Kent. "They've got a big cathedral, and I think all priests and monks live there."

"Are you taking me home?" I asked Miss Day.

"No, you are going to a place in Kent called Greenacres. It's a remand home… It's only temporary."

"How temporary?"

"Maybe a month, then you will appear at the Junior Court in Chatham. It will be up to the judge were you go from there."

The old Victorian building was very grey, dark and cold-looking. It was run by ex-coppers, both male and female.

It was more like a prison because every door was locked behind us. I was frightened out of my life.

A man opened the door to us. He was wearing black trousers with a bunch of keys attached to his trouser belt. His white sleeveless shirt showed off his muscles. His black hair looked dyed, and so did his moustache that curled up at both ends.

We followed him into a large hallway to book me in.

Just then, two girls were being dragged through the hall from another room. One of the girl's faces was bleeding, and she was holding her nose with her hand. Her clothes were covered in blood. She was calling the other girl a fat, ugly bitch, as well as other names. The oldest girl, who was around sixteen and looked like Giant Haystacks the professional wrestler, knocked the ex-policeman who was trying to restrain her to the floor.

Alarm bells went off as other officers ran into the hallway. About six in all took her down to her knees. She was handcuffed and led away through another door, still giving them a line of curses.

I stood frozen to the spot with horror.

Everyone here is mad, I thought. My sister Libby was right… I've ended up in a nuthouse! But why was I here, in prison? *I was only trying to protect myself from my father. All I did was run away, I've not killed no one.*

"Why can't I go to another children's home?" I asked Miss Day.

"We've only got a few homes in Kent, and there is no room for you at the moment," she replied.

"Then send me somewhere else. It don't have to be Kent."

She said her farewells and more or less ran out of the building.

I was handed over to a girl called Katie Wells. She told me she was a lesbian. *A bit strange,* I thought, *her telling me her birth sign.*

"Oh, that's nice," I said, "I'm a Capricorn," trying to be polite back.

She gave me a weird kind of look.

I followed her into a quite large front room. About thirty girls were sat around the room playing cards, others talking, or watching television.

"This is Bridie," Katie said.

Everyone looked over in my direction but said nothing. I was the first to break the silence.

"What's for supper? Does anyone know?" One of the girls asked whether I liked soul.

"No," I replied. "I don't like fish." Everyone burst out laughing.

"Gloria is talking about soul music… Aretha Franklin, James Brown…" said Katie.

I didn't have a clue who she was talking about and said so.

"Why are you here?" asked Gloria.

"I am called a runaway by the Social Services," I said.

"Running from what?" she asked.

"None of your business." The room went very quiet.

Gloria came toward me. I can't remember which part of her obese body reached me first. Before I knew what was happening, her ten-ton body was on top of me. I didn't know what was worse – her weight pushing me through the floorboards or the stench of her body odour. The smell was sickening.

It took four girls to get the fat pig off of me. I brushed myself down and turned to walk away, but she pulled me back towards her and raised her hand to slap me, so I head butted her in the face. Blood poured from her face. Two cops ran into the room and looked at Ten-Ton-Tess laying on the floor, pretending she was dead.

I was handcuffed and led away to a small room with no windows, a scruffy-looking mattress on the floor that I assumed was to be my bed, a grey blanket on the bed, and no pillow. A piss bucket stood in the corner of the room.

"You are a hard little cow, aren't you?" said the screw.

"No, I am not. I just won't let others beat up on me ever again."

"Well," she said, "you will be allowed to empty your bucket twice a day, and three times a day, your food will be slotted through the hatch of the door."

"How long will I be in here?" I asked her as she took the handcuffs off me.

This is only my first day. What is going to happen to me before I leave this hellhole? I was thinking to myself.

The door slammed shut. I hated confinement but it didn't bother me being on my own. I could be in a crowded room and still feel alone, but in my secret garden, night after night, I wasn't by myself. I had Sister Bernadette and all the children who were lost to their parents. I found it very bizarre that the children never got any older – even my brother Paul Roy was still an infant in arms, but I was ageing.

A week after I was freed from the punishing room, all the other girls wanted to be my friend. Why, I had no idea, but Gloria kept well away from me. I didn't fancy being locked up over her again.

Katie was a good mate. She had been running away from her abusive dad from the age of ten. The police would find her and take her back home to him every time. She didn't tell them what he was doing to her because he told her he would kill her mum if she did, so she kept quiet.

Even though Katie confided in me, I didn't think I could truly trust her or anyone else. Her father was from my area, and her mother was a white Irish Catholic woman. She wouldn't believe her daughter's allegations about her husband sexually abusing her. Katie said she was about six years old when he first raped her. It was proven by the police in court and he got ten years in jail for his crime, but her mother still blamed her for her father's wrongdoing – *A bit like my mother,* I thought.

I liked Katie a lot. She was nothing like some of the other girls in the home who sniffed lighter fuel, nail polish, or any other common household product, even hairspray, just to get high. I'm sure the governors knew what the girls were getting up to, but chose to turn a blind eye to what was happening around them. It made the screws' lives and work easier for them.

The old judge looked down at me from the bench. His gold-looking glasses kept slipping down his small nose, and he was getting aggravated at having to keep pushing them back up. His grey hair and moustache curled up at both ends, which I though looked ridiculous.

"Now, my dear girl," he said in his squeaky voice. "What I am going to do now is for your own good. I am placing you under a care order until you are eighteen years old. Do you understand?"

I didn't. I kept silent.

He continued to say that my poor parents could not tolerate my bad behaviour around them and the other children.

"*My* behaviour! Is he having a laugh?" I said to my social worker.

"Be quiet," she said. "You'll get your chance to say something when he asks you to."

I just couldn't believe what my parents had written in a statement about me – things like I didn't help Mother out with home chores, that I constantly kept hitting my brothers and sisters, that I was given pocket money every week, and that I was always running around with boys. The only boys I knew were my little brothers.

I wanted to tell the old judge the truth about my parents, but I knew he wouldn't believe me. He would think I was spiteful towards them. As for them giving any of my siblings or me pocket money! Yeh, right! They wouldn't give us their licking off their arse, let alone money for doing nothing in the house. Mother must have forgotten I had to scrub the wooden stairs every morning and, after I had taken the young siblings to school, clean their bedrooms. Even our Jeremy, who believed he was in some way related to Elvis Presley, used me as his dosser. I was forever making him cups of bloody tea, washing his outfits for work as a barman in our local pub, cleaning his messy bedroom, running to the shops to get his tobacco. He didn't give me a thank you for doing any of his shitty chores. He was brought up with the opinion that women and girls were not superior to men. It was a woman's place to wait on him hand and foot.

No wonder his girlfriend fucked him off out of it after four years together. He came home with his tail between his legs, telling Father she was a useless woman. A chauvinistic pig, that's all he was, and I disliked him.

I was delighted when the judge said I would not be going home. I think he expected me to burst into tears. No such luck.

My only concern was that my sister Nancy was living at home, and I knew I had to get her away from Father. Mrs Carter, who was going to be my new social worker, was taking me to my new dwelling in Southampton. She asked if I was all right away from my family. I told her that Father was sending Nancy out stealing for him. He wasn't, but I hoped that by telling her a lie, she would take Nancy away from my parents. She had a look of horror on her face. She reminded me of Olive out of 'Popeye'.

After some weeks of being in the Southampton home with nuns again, I found out Nancy was still at home with my parents. I just couldn't understand why Olive Oyl didn't look into my concerns about my sister. I was so worried about her. I couldn't eat or sleep with bad thoughts playing riot with my brain. Night after night I could see him hurting her.

Please God, take away what I think is happening to my sister Nancy, I would cry.

A few weeks before I was sent away, Mother had beaten the shit out of her because she hadn't made her bed. The hand brush she hit her with broke into pieces. I was screaming at Mother to stop, but she wouldn't.

I learnt later from Nancy that she had told Mother about Father trying to do his dirty deeds on her again. She thought by telling her again, Mother would believe her this time. Why Nancy would think this was beyond me.

I decided to do a runner from home. My plan was if I could get back to Chatham where my parents lived, without them knowing I was about, I could grab Nancy and take her away with me. Where to I didn't know, but at least she'd be safe.

I told my plan to Wendy, who I had become friends with at home. She couldn't keep her mouth shut for long because by the evening, three other girls knew I was planning to escape.

Sarah Green, who was apparently perfect and had the privilege of putting out the trash every night after dinner, was trusted with the backdoor keys to do her job. *Perhaps she is perfect,* I thought; *there's my escape route.* She was desperate to see her boyfriend, who had not written to her in months. She needed to find out why. She was four years older than me, quite attractive in some ways, with her red hair and green eyes. The whole of her body was full of freckles – a sign of beauty, she would say.

Vanessa was tall as a giant and so skinny because she had some eating disease. Everything she had eaten during the day she would puke back up by shoving her fingers down her throat. Just hearing her do that made me gag. I didn't realise until much later the seriousness of her illness. She ended up killing herself.

Olivia claimed to be a witch and would spend her days trying to convince everyone she had magic powers. I told her one day that if she had magical powers, why hadn't she made herself invisible and got out of the home a long time ago? She'd been there for over a year. She didn't answer the question but instead said she had turned Sister Anna into a toad. Looking at the nun's face, I could believe that.

After being cooped up in that home for a month, with the outside world forbidden to me, the cold December night's breeze was a welcome feeling to my face. The stars shone like large diamonds in the sky. God, I felt so happy to be free again.

Hitchhiking Horror

We walked for miles before we got a lift from an old couple who asked where we were heading.

"I'm going to Kent… Don't know where the others are going."

"We're making our way to Shepherd's Bush if that helps you."

"That'll be fine," I replied, not having a clue where Shepherd's Bush was.

The four of us squeezed into the Mini Cooper. The journey was uncomfortable because I was crushed to death in the back by the others.

Olivia took off her Dr Martens boots, complaining that the back of her heels were hurting and that her boots were cutting into her flesh. The smell of her feet was disgusting. A mixture of rotten cabbages and sweat seemed to linger in the air. The old woman wasn't amused, and she asked who had passed wind and would whoever it was kindly refrain from doing it again as she suffered from asthma and felt an attack coming on. She put her red silk scarf over her nose and mouth as she pulled down the car window to let the repulsive odour out.

Sarah took to a fit of giggles as she let out a very noisy fart. It sounded like a duck in agony. The stench was something else.

The old man wasn't amused. He pulled his car over and told us to get out and fuck off as he drove away, leaving us standing in the rain.

It didn't bother me that it was very cold, as I had on my warm winter coat and grey tights with my black Dr Martens boots that Social Services had bought for me. I didn't feel sorry for the others, who were shivering because they were dressed as if they were going to the beach, as it was still summer, so dresses, cardigans, bare legs and flat shoes were the norm, but I felt comfort being wrapped up in layers, regardless the weather, and Olivia clearly took comfort from her smelly Dr Martens.

We continued walking for some time. A lorry pulled up beside us. "Jump in, girls. Where are you heading?" asked the driver.

"We are going to Kent."

"So am I," he said.

We all got in without hesitation and were glad to be out of the rain. "Don't you know how dangerous it is for pretty girls like yourselves to be hitchhiking?"

None of us replied to his question. I whispered to Wendy that he gave me the creeps.

"Don't be stupid, Bridie. There is four of us and one of him. Do you think he's going to do anything to us? Relax, settle down, and enjoy the journey. You'll be home soon," said Wendy.

I made sure I sat near the door with my face up against the window, just in case, I thought.

The driver was around fifty years old, had a bald head, and was very fat. When he smiled, I could see he was toothless. *Probably Wendy was right,* I thought; he looked harmless.

I closed my eyes just to rest them for a few moments. With the heat of the cab, the roaring of the engine, and the cassette player playing sad country & western music, I fell into a deep sleep.

When I opened them again, it was morning. Still raining. I looked over at the driver, expecting to see him still stuffing his face with sweets as he had been doing before I fell asleep, but to my surprise, another man was doing the driving. Surely I would have known if we had stopped.

I nudged Wendy, who was still asleep. She, in turn, poked Sarah awake.

"Did we stop last night?" I asked him. "Where is our mate?"

He didn't reply.

"Where is Olivia?" I asked again. That was not her real name – Valencia was her name. Why she'd decided to call herself Olivia was beyond me.

I hadn't noticed before, but a curtain was hanging up between the driver's seat and ours. My stomach was having the strange feeling it got when something bad was going to happen or had happened.

"Not to worry, pal, she is just resting," said the driver, who said his name was Luke.

"Olivia!" I called out.

No answer.

Again I called out her name. Still nothing.

Sarah turned to go look behind the curtain and let out a scream. I was frozen, I couldn't look, but Wendy had got up on her knees and was trying to drag The toothless man off of Sarah, he managed to get his hand over Sarah's mouth and her arm up her back, trying to hold her down.

"Get off her!" Wendy yelled at him, jumping on his back.

He let go of Sarah and grabbed Wendy by her throat. Wendy managed somehow to kick him in the bollocks, leaving him in agony.

"Jesus!" cried Sarah, looking down under the cab bed at Olivia, who was bound by her hands and legs and stripped from her waist down. White tape was over her mouth. No wonder she couldn't call out for help.

Out of the corner of my eye, beside the bed, I saw a small baseball bat. Picking it up, I kept hitting him on the back with it. The toothless one was yelling out for his mate to stop the lorry and to fucking kill us. His mate Luke didn't stop, so I kept hitting him with the bat until the other girls helped Olivia up and got her dressed.

The blood was pouring from the toothless man's head. Once he flaked out, I stopped hitting him. Thinking I had killed him, I sat trembling with the weapon still in my hand. Splashes of his blood were on my new coat and boots, and anger was running wild through my mind with flashbacks of what Father had done to me and my sister Nancy.

I dropped the bat, realising what I had done.

"Jesus! I've killed him," I cried. "God, please forgive me. I was only trying to help my friend," I heard myself say.

"Stop babbling," Wendy said. "He can't help you."

"Now, we got to get this bastard to stop the fucking truck," said Sarah, picking up the blood-stained bat from the floor and holding it to Luke, the driver's head, Slim Whitman's song 'Rose Marie' was playing full blast on the radio. God, we couldn't believe what had gone on in the back of that lorry.

We all fixed our gaze on Luke. Staring down at him with a no-nonsense look, Sarah yelled, "Stop the fucking lorry, you son of a bitch!"

With the bat held high over his head, Luke, who was much younger than his friend, the toothless wonder, quickly decided he didn't fancy taking on four maniac girls, or the bloodstained bat aimed at his head.

"I can't just pull over on the motorway!"

"You can and you will," said Sarah, pushing the bat into the back of his neck.

He pulled over without hesitation. We pushed Olivia, who was still sobbing hard, out of the lorry first and the rest of us followed, before Luke, or whatever his name was – somehow I didn't believe that was his name – drove away with his half-mullered pal.

He yelled he was going to find us, and when he did, he was going to kill us.

I wasn't bothered by his threats. Once the police knew we half-murdered the toothless twat, I'd be thrown in prison and probably executed anyway, I thought.

"Look!" said Wendy, pointing at the lorry. "Old Gummy is still alive!"

I looked up to see the toothless one with his head sticking out of the passenger-side window, waving his fist at us as the lorry sped away along the road.

We managed to cross over the dual carriageway to walk on the other side of the motorway. We felt it would be safer, just in case those animals decided to wait at the top of the road for us.

The fog had lifted, but it was still very cold. Wendy pulled a few dock leaves from the verge and began wiping them down my coat to get the blood spots off.

We continued to walk for a while, refusing to take any other lifts. We didn't have a clue where we were until we saw a sign saying Farthing Corner Services near Gillingham, Kent. We went in and sat down. Olivia took her boots off. This time none of us complained about her smelly feet.

Wendy asked her what she was doing behind the curtain in the first place, and why didn't she wake us up before she had gone behind it?

Olivia said that the gummy man had asked her to do him a favour by getting his bottle of water from his bed behind the curtain. She said all she could remember was bending down to pick the bottle up and that she knew she had been hit with something at the back of her head and then a hand over her mouth, and that was it. She must have blacked out. When she came around, he was raping her, and there was no way out. With her hands and legs tied and her mouth gagged with tape, she couldn't cry out for help. He'd fallen asleep on top of her and she just couldn't move, and the rest we knew.

"Jesus," said Wendy. "Do you think they were planning to kill all four of us?"

"Who knows. At least we are free from them," I groaned.

Olivia was still crying when two women came over to our table and asked if she was all right. The blonde-headed woman asked if we would like a drink or something.

"Coke, please," Sarah said.

"Is that four Cokes?"

We nodded our heads.

The woman who stayed at the table with us was asking too many questions for our liking. Where did we live? What school did we go to? How old were we?

Wendy asked her if she was a policewoman and why all the questions. "I am only concerned," she replied.

"No need to be," I said.

Wendy and I took ourselves off to the toilets. Looking in the mirror, we could see why she was being nosey. Our hair was sticking up all over the place and I had a few spots of blood on my face and hands. We cleaned ourselves up and returned to our table to find not only Cokes waiting for us but sandwiches as well.

None of us had the stomach to eat them after what we had been through. Food was the last thing on our minds.

I told the woman we had been in a fight with some girls over a few boys. I think they believed us because both of them smiled at us and said no men or boys were worth fighting over.

We scrambled out of the building as quickly as we could, hoping the two busy-bodies didn't change their minds and call the police on us.

I knew I wasn't far from my parents' home and decided it would be best if I continued my journey on my own. Wendy was having none of it. She was going with me, just in case something else happened. At least we'd have each other to talk to and look out for one another.

Wendy reminded me of Katie in the remand home – feeling obligated to look after me. I wasn't a twit, just a bit naive of the ways of the world, but I was learning fast.

Sarah and Olivia were going to Maidstone because Sarah had some relations there. We hugged each other farewell. I couldn't or didn't want to let go of Olivia, who was still trembling and crying over her evil ordeal with the gummy man. I didn't dare cry with her like the other girls, because I knew I would never stop. I knew how she was feeling. I had been through the same experience and pain that she was feeling right now, as if someone had reached inside your soul and forced it to die slowly. It didn't matter how many baths you had; you never felt clean. You are numb, and no one can fix you. I will never be that innocent little child again, like Olivia will never be the same person she was before going on this journey.

"I wish you had killed him," Olivia said in a croaky voice. I kissed her cheek, and we parted.

We were only two streets away from my parents' house when a police car pulled us up and asked for our names. Of course, we didn't give them our real ones. Then a policewoman got out of the car and put handcuffs on us. I asked politely why they were doing this to us; we'd done nothing wrong.

The policeman said they believed we were two of the girls who had run away from a children's home in Southampton. I took all the wicked oaths under the sun that he was mistaking us for others, but once he'd showed us pictures of ourselves that the fucking nuns had provided them with, we knew the game was up.

We were bungled into the back of the car, then taken to Chatham police station and put in separate rooms.

I was asked about the other two girls that they were still looking for.

I completely denied being with them and told them I was making my way home because my sister Nancy wasn't well, and she needed me. They informed me that she was taken into care after running away from home on too many occasions to look for me.

I cried with happiness, knowing that that bastard of a father couldn't put his filthy hands on her ever again. I wasn't allowed to know her whereabouts in case we ran off together.

I was put in a cell with the door open until the next morning when a social worker came to take me to a home in Maidstone, but I refused to go with him. I could see by his face that he was getting fed up with trying to persuade me to go with him. *After what had happened to Olivia, no way was I going anywhere with a stranger,* I thought.

"Where's my old social worker, Olive Oyl?"

"She's on maternity leave."

He saw the puzzled look on my face and stepped in to tell me that she was expecting a baby.

"Wow! She's having a baby Popeye!"

He smiled at me, thinking he had won me over. He was wrong. I wasn't going anywhere with him.

He stayed in the police station for the next four hours, talking to me as if he'd known me for years. I knew his life story before his replacement turned up, and he still didn't know anything about me, only what was in the few papers in his folder.

"Hello, Bridget... Or would you prefer to be called Bridie?"

"Call me whatever you like," I replied.

"I am Mrs Bristol, your new social worker. How did you manage to get this far?"

"We hitchhiked."

"How many lifts did you manage to get?"

"Just the one from a very old couple. Why are you asking me these questions?"

A policewoman came into the cell and sat on a chair. Her arse had caught my attention, as it was so large it was hanging off either side of the chair. I was wondering if the chair would break under the strain..

"Can you explain to me why you and Wendy had a lot of splatters of blood on your clothing?" asked the policewoman.

Shit, I thought. Wendy had opened her big mouth, after we had all made a deal to say nothing. Olivia had begged us not to. She'd said if the toothless one happened to die of his head injury, we would all swing on a rope because we'd helped to kill him.

"Best you go and ask Wendy," I said.

I didn't want any rope around my neck strangling me. I'd seen my sister Libby after she'd tried to do herself in, and she didn't look a pretty sight.

"We asked Wendy and don't believe her story about saving a dog. I suppose you are going to tell us the same cock and bull tale of rubbish?"

"I don't know if she told you the whole story."

The policewoman grabbed her pen and notebook, eager to get my statement.

"We were walking down the street – I didn't see the name of it because it was too dark – Wendy needed a poo. She was behind the bushes. She must had been shitting for some time. Anyway, the sky just lit up all around us."

"What kind of lights?"

"How the fuck would I know? What I know is, it was just lights."

I was trying to make myself look big by swearing like Wendy did. Every other word she said was a swear word. People seemed to back away from her when she cursed at them. I was hoping Fatty and the goggle-eyed policewoman would do the same with me. They knew I was lying, but I continued telling them my story anyway.

"We both got scared. We couldn't move with fear. I think they were flying saucers or helicopters. Whatever they were, we were terrified."

"I suppose you are going to tell us you saw little green men," said the policewoman.

"Actually, no, but they hadn't landed," I said.

The policewoman stopped writing and looked at me with misaligned eyes.

I pretended to cry. Peeping through my fingers, I could see my pretend tears weren't having any effect on the two women.

"I reckon Wendy was really scared. But how would I know? I am not a mind-reader," I said, rolling my eyes. "We heard something like a bump, a savage wild animal was whining, and that's when we found the poor dog. And realised the UFO must have landed after all, on top of the poor dog. We did try to save it. I pumped its belly, whilst Wendy give it the kiss of life. That's how we got blood on our clothes. That's the truth, the whole truth, and nothing but the truth."

I remembered having to say words similar when I had to give evidence in court against my father. The judge somehow knew I was lying when I said it had been my sister who'd beaten us up, but he'd looked down kindly on me because he could see the fear in my face.

My interrogation was over. Both women left my cell shaking their heads at me. They were looking for the truth, but wouldn't be getting it from me.

I was hoping I could see Wendy, but she had already left the police station with her probation officer. I never saw her again or knew what happened to her. I felt so guilty about falling asleep that night, thinking if only I had stayed awake, just maybe what had happened to Olivia might not have taken place.

I don't think the sick bastards reported us to the police or that the toothless one died because the police didn't push the subject to how we got blood all over us. My only real regret that night was that I didn't kill the scumbag for Olivia's sake.

St Mary's School

St Mary's School for Young Ladies was an old convent that had been turned into a home for wayward girls. The nuns believed that once their pupils were ready to be released back into the world again after three years, we would be young women with clean minds, not sinners, and maybe one or two would become nuns as well.

The routine was very hard: up at six every morning to go to Mass, breakfast at eight, cleaning the dormitories at nine, school from ten till twelve, then laundry work from one until six in the evening.

I worked in the laundry five days a week, and bloody hated it. The noise of the machines was deafening. We were treated like little slaves. My job was to put the sheets in the red-hot, heavy rolling machines that dried them. I would often get burns on my hands and arms while feeding them through. We never got paid for the hard work we had to do for the nuns.

If I wasn't working in the laundry, I had to work in their chocolate factory making moneyboxes. We had to assemble the boxes. The plastic boxes were to encourage youngsters to save their pocket money if they were lucky enough to receive any.

Once they were put together, little squares of Cadbury's milk chocolate were put in the back of them: you would put a penny in the slot, and a little chocolate would fall out of the bottom, if it was working properly.

Sometimes a large order would come into the convent; then we worked the weekend as well until we had finished the order. We only got five minutes' break every four hours. We were given the choice of a glass of water or tea to drink, and a few mangy old biscuits to eat, but at least we had the evening meal to look forward to. Some days the food would be quite good – sausage and chips was my favourite meal of the week, with luscious tomato sauce poured over them. Yummy! Followed by a cup of tea that looked and tasted like cat's piss.

We weren't allowed to speak to each other whilst at meals or working. If anyone was caught, they'd be hit on the head with the nuns' rulers.

I hated working in the laundry and factory in the summer months. The heat was unbearable. The sweat would be pouring off our bodies, and our faces looked like we were out too long in the sun: nothing further from the truth, as we hardly saw the light of day. Many times I witnessed girls fainting because of the heat. The nuns would slap their faces to bring them around and give them a cup of water. Once the girls were feeling well enough, they'd be put back to work.

I often felt sorry for myself. I'd cry in bed, telling myself that I was only trying to keep myself and Nancy safe, and if that was wrong in society, then society could go and fuck itself.

I remember when I first arrived at the home, thinking it would be just the same as the other ones I had been in. I didn't have to work long hours for my keep. Yes, I did a lot of housework, but I did that when I was living with my parents, plus I liked to keep things neat and tidy around me, so I wasn't too bothered about the smell of disinfectant.

I was taken into a small room, told to strip to my knickers, and was given a new outfit; a long, patterned dress, grey jumper, white ankle socks and brown sandals. I wouldn't see my own clothes for two years until I was leaving the convent. Everything I owned was taken off me, not that I had anything, just the clothes I was standing in and my silver holy medal that I bought one of my brothers for Christmas many years back. It was my reminder that I'd had someone who'd cared for me and loved me. In my lonely hours, I would hold onto it for dear life and imagine the three of us running the streets of Manchester again, getting up to all the mischief that we did. God, I missed them.

The nun seized me by my elbow and more or less dragged me into the dining room. "Sit down here," she said, pointing to a chair next to a girl who smiled at me.

I looked around the table: six other girls dressed just alike. All looked at me with friendly faces. Once we'd introduced ourselves to each other, they informed me about all the dos and don'ts of the rules we all had to abide by. Jacqueline, who was sitting next to me, stank of BO. She was very large in stature, and her afro hair looked like it was never washed, let alone combed. I wasn't quite sure which was the biggest… her nostrils or her mouth. Her narrow eyes looked me up and down as she asked me if I was going to eat the bread and marmite the nun had put in front of me. "No," I said and slipped it over to her. She shoved the whole slice into her mouth and smiled at me. The marmite stuck to her teeth, blending in with their already brown tinge of a colour, as if she had been eating shit.

I was feeling sick and was sure the thing that was making me feel that way was the stink coming from Jacqueline Brown's body.

My nose wouldn't stop itching. I kept sneezing across the room. Sister Margaret Mary, with her long Pinocchio nose, and Sister Luke, with her beady eyes, were staring over at me.

"Whoops!" said Jacqueline. "Looks like you're in trouble." She had a sly grin on her face.

I just couldn't keep my eyes off her while she ran her tongue over, what looked like her shit-stained buck teeth.

"I did nothin' wrong," I said.

Sister Margaret Mary asked if I was doing drugs, and what was I hiding up my nose. "Nothing," I replied.

Sister Luke grabbed me by my hair, pulled my head backwards, and began poking about inside my nose with her bony finger. She shoved it so far up my nose that it began to bleed.

"What the hell do you expect to be up there?" I screamed at her.

She slapped me across the face, so I kicked her in the leg. I didn't get a chance to tell them that it was the disgusting odour from Jacqueline Brown's body that was making me sneeze.

"Get your witchy hands off me!" I yelled at Sister Margaret Mary, who dragged me out to the hallway and shoved me into a cupboard and locked it.

I couldn't stand up in it, it was so small.

"You ugly pig!" I called out at her. "Fuck you! May you and the rest of your cronies rot in Hell!"

Be calm, I was telling myself, *be calm.* By doing this, I felt it would stop me from going insane. It was pitch-black darkness, and I could hear my heart pumping in my ears. The cupboard smelled of damp and smelly socks. For a moment, I felt I was back in the punishing room in the convent in Ireland, but without the bottles of wine, of course. At least that had shutters that I could open and let the light into the room.

What is wrong with nuns? Why do they always lock us in cupboards? Maybe they were locked up in them themselves when they were kids. That's why they are so small in height. It stunted their growth, I thought.

I don't know how long I had been kept in there, but once I was let out, it was dark outside through the hallway windows. My body felt as stiff as a poker for sitting in the same position for such a long time.

"Come with me," said Sister Jane, who was walking with a limp.

I wondered how many times she had been shoved away to end up with a gammy leg.

I followed her up a flight of stairs to a dormitory with seven single beds.

"This is your bed," she said, pointing to the empty bed in the far corner of the room.

As I lay down on the lumpy mattress, my only thoughts were that if this was my first day here, what do the next three years have for me? Nothing but cruelty. I've got to keep my mouth shut and work out a way to escape from here.

"Are you okay?" A voice came out of the dark.

I recognised the voice right away. It was smelly Jacqueline. Jesus! As if my life wasn't hard enough. Now I've got to share the room with a stinking skunk. I didn't reply to her.

I pulled the stiff white sheet over my head and tried to sleep. It was impossible. My mind kept racing from one thing to another. I couldn't even get into my secret garden. God, what was happening to me? Maybe, people who don't get enough natural light, lose brain function? Yes, that's what was wrong – my brain had given up. It had gone dead.

For weeks and months on end, I felt numb and had a feeling that I had fallen into a very deep, dark hole and couldn't get myself out. I didn't know what was making me feel that way, so I put it all down to Jacqueline Brown,. I had convinced myself that something nasty from her stinking body had entered my brain, and that's why my head was always feeling foggy. Even the nuns had said in one of their religious classes that a lot of the girls in the home had demons – demons of drink, demons of sex, demons of lying, demons of stealing, demons of lust. *Fucking hell, the place is full of them, and now I've got demons of Jacqueline Brown's BO.*

At Sunday Service, Father O'Grady was going to bless us all with holy water and purify us all from the devils that lived within our souls.

Father O'Grady was a small man with a bald head and black, bushy eyebrows that looked like large, hairy caterpillars. When he laughed, which was often, he sounded like an old donkey in distress, but all the girls seemed to like him.

During Mass, he walked around all the benches, sprinkling holy water over the girls. When he came to where I was sitting, I grabbed the silver-looking bowl out of his hands and poured what was left of the water over my own head, believing that if I did have demons, I had drowned them now or at least God might wash Jacqueline's bloody armpits.

Everyone gasped with horror as they looked at me with disbelieving faces.

One of the nuns grabbed me by my cardigan and led me out of the church, but the old priest intervened and took me by the hand and led me to a small room at the back of the altar.

"Sit here," he said, "until the service is over." He gave me a towel to wipe my hair. "Stop crying. I'll be with you shortly," he said.

It had been many years since I'd genuinely cried, but lately I couldn't stop it. All the emotion, sorrow and pain was releasing itself from me all at once, it seemed. I was still whingeing when the priest returned.

"Now, my girl. What is this about? Why would you do such a thing?"

I explained to him about believing that Jacqueline Brown's demon must have jumped from her and crawled up my nostrils and was messing about with my head.

Father O'Grady laughed. "What nonsense! What is the matter with you, girl?"

"I just told you, Father. Wasn't you listening?" I asked him.

"How old are you?"

"Just fourteen."

"What's your name?"

"Bridie," I said.

"Why are you here?"

"Because you brought me in here."

"No, I mean in the convent."

"I am a runaway."

"From where?"

"Anywhere," I replied.

"Can you tell me why you keep running away from whatever place you go?" I didn't answer him.

He stopped filling in the information form and looked at me. His eyebrows were jet black, whilst the few strands of hair that stuck up on his head were completely grey.

"I am obliged to pass on all information, but if you'd like me to hear your confession, I would not be able to reveal it to the Reverend Mother. I promise you this in God's honour."

I broke down in tears and told all. The lorry men's violent attack on a friend, but didn't give her name. "I didn't kill him when I attacked him with his own baseball bat, but I wish I had."

"How do you know you didn't kill him?" the priest asked.

"Because he had his head out of the lorry spitting at us as they passed by on the other side of the motorway," I sobbed.

"Where is your friend now?"

"I believe she's with her family, but I don't know."

He listened to my story, sympathetically. As he took my hand, I pulled it away.

"God forgives you. Now, say ten Hail Marys and ten Our Fathers for your penance."

After I had said all the prayers, he said my sins were forgiven. Can't say I felt any better with all that palaver and gobbledygook, but at least I knew the priest couldn't report back to the witchy nuns about the conversation we'd had.

Sister Heather seized me by my elbow and pushed me forward. "Sit down here," she said, pointing to a chair.

A girl about seventeen years old sat next to me. She smiled. "Get scraping these potatoes," Sister Heather hissed at us.

On the floor next to us was a large tin bath overflowing with spuds for us to scrub. "What are we feeding today, the five thousand?"

"No," said the girl. "Three times a year, we have to cook for all the old folks in the village."

"Why is that?" I asked.

"Did you know that the Catholic Church is one of the richest churches in the world?" she asked.

How the fuck would I know that, and what has that got to do with us having to do the nuns' work for them? I thought.

"That's nice of them, to feed the poor people," I replied.

"Nice? Are you for fucking real? They're not helping the unfortunate old-age pensioners… It's their donations they're after!"

"Donations?"

"The church roof, the new extension to the nuns' quarters over the years…"

"Shut up!" said Lilly Doherty, one of the older girls in charge. "Get on with your work."

"You, girl," said Sister Jane, pointing her long finger at me, "Follow me."

I couldn't stand the old crow. I walked behind her and watched her fat arse wiggling from one side to the other in rhythm with her footsteps. She may have only been five foot nothing, but did she have a punch behind that small frame of hers. I felt her strength one day when I refused to go to the factory to work. The cramps in my stomach were unbearable. I was losing so much blood because of my periods, I could have donated a few pints to the hospitals. She grabbed me off the chair by my hair. I lashed out at her, pulling the veil off her head. Jesus! Her bald head looked like a dumpling with a pair of ears stuck to it. She gave me an almighty punch that sent me halfway up the polished hallway and split my bottom lip. Seeing the commotion, two other nuns ran to her rescue. Yeh, ran to *her* rescue: I was the one up the floor, bleeding out. I was thrown into a small cupboard once again. By now, it felt like my second home.

It was the middle of January when Sister Mary called me aside. "Get yourself tidied up. You got visitors."

"Who?" I asked.

"Never you mind. Move it! You should count yourself lucky that we have allowed you any visitation. It's only the large, kind donation we received from them that we decided just the once wouldn't be a problem. After all, a donation is a donation," said Sister Mary.

I sat puzzled in the waiting room, wondering who it could be.

I could hear footsteps. Someone was dragging their feet behind them. I didn't know anyone with a gammy leg, I thought. The door opened. I hardly dared look up, so I kept my eyes focused on the wooden floor.

My father and grandfather stood in the doorway. Both stared at me. I was dumbfounded.

What are they doing here? Has someone died? I asked myself.

My tongue suddenly died. I couldn't speak as Father smiled at me.

"Hi," I said to Grandad, who looked very grey and had aged since I last saw him in Manchester. The blue veins that seemed to be running through his face made it look transparent. His once blue sparkling eyes had lost their sparkle. He told me he had been run over some years back and both of his legs were broken, hence the limp and walking sticks.

When I could finally find the will, through the shock. to have a conversation, I asked how my grandma was.

"Oh, her… she ran off with a mansheen, black as the ace of spades. Well, he wasn't born black, but may as well have been. The fecker was a coalman."

He may have looked half-dead, but he still had his wacky sense of humour. I couldn't help laughing with him.

"What happened to Bimbo?"

"She took the cross-eyed dog with her. She loved that flea-ridden thing more than me."

I could see tears welling up in his eyes and gave him a cuddle, saying, don't worry, she'd come back to him.

"It's been two fecking years now, my girl. She's taking her time or got lost on her way back," Grandad moaned. "Anyway, I didn't come to discuss her. Your father said you are training to be a nun."

"Me? A nun?" I couldn't help bursting out laughing at the suggestion. "I am here because I am a runner."

"A fecking runner!" he cried. "By the time you're twenty years old, your bones and joints would have given out. Look for another career!"

He continued to tell me I was as ugly as I used to be. *Straight to the point as always,* I thought.

"Yes, I could see you as a nurse," he decided.

"Grandad, why have you come?"

"I am dying, my girl. Doctors say maybe a few months, but you are with the holy nuns. You could ask them to say a Mass for me."

"Of course, I will, but what are you dying of?"

"I got the Big C," he said.

"What's that?"

"Girl, if you are going to be a nurse, best you start reading medical books. It's cancer, fecking cancer," he replied.

I didn't have the heart to tell him I couldn't read and had no desire to work as a nurse, I hated blood. I looked over at my father, who had a blank expression on his face and wished it was him who was going to leave the earth, not my grandad. I just couldn't bring myself to talk to the creep.

The door opened. It was one of the nuns to tell us our time was up. "Take this," Grandad said, handing me a white envelope.

I didn't have a clue why he gave it to me, especially if there were donations for the convent inside.

Grandad kissed and cuddled me goodbye. I knew in my heart that that would be the last time I would see him. He passed away a few weeks later. I didn't know how this affected my father but knew Mother would be devastated. She loved the old chuck dearly.

Sister Joan took me and my letter to the Mother Superior's office. "Did you enjoy your time with your family?" asked Mother Superior.

I was just going to say that my grandad would like a Mass said for him…

"Never mind that, hand me the envelope. Is your grandad a wealthy man?" she asked.

"I wouldn't know. Grandma always said he was an old Scrooge," I replied.

I could see the disappointed look on her square-looking face.

She said, "I see your grandma was right. Not one penny to help for your keep."

I work six days a week for my bloody keep, I thought, but kept my feelings to myself. I didn't fancy being put in the cupboard again.

Sister Joan read the letter out loud. I couldn't understand why he had written most of it in Gaelic Cant, the Irish Travellers' language that folks called the secret language, with a touch of English.

I thought there was something he was trying to tell me in secret and didn't want the nuns knowing. Try as I might, I couldn't find any code.

Dia Lakin,
Glordhna' bi teign lushing like your *gathera* and *nederm. Na' bl taring* to
any *sublas* are musing of with them. Focal *diahal Tremlach* of them.
Is *mise ag* fail *'bhar's den aunt'se. Ledo tholla ra'gul'* for *mise.*
Maith is *mise* not leaving *duit* any *gairead. Ta beoir krosh* it all.
N a-dean dearmao orm.
Go raibh mal'th agat! And *Slainte! Mhaith.* May *dhaluin* bless *tu'*
Seanathair
XX

He was telling me not to be a drunk like Father and Mother and warning
me to keep away from boys, saying the majority of them were dirty devils.

No fear of that, I thought, but why was he suggesting that to me anyway?
I was only fourteen years old and had never been with a boy. The only men
around the home were the priest and the gardener, who was as old as the hills
and walked with a limp. He was training Jacqueline Brown to be a landscape
gardener; she was good at organising plants and things. The nuns were hoping
that once the old fellow retired, she would stay in the home and be their
gardener, with very little pay.

The nuns were quite happy having her out of their way for a few hours a
day. She suffered from disgusting body odour. No matter how many showers
she had, her body still stank.

Jacqueline didn't mind working with Mr Cooper. She called him her
fuckbuddy and liked to thread the needle with him.

I didn't have a clue what she was on about – I thought at the time that he
was teaching her to sew, as well as garden.

Grandad also said that he was leaving me no money – it was going to a
new woman he had only just met twelve months before he died. It didn't
bother me one way or another, but leaving Grandma nothing… After years of
suffering from his womanising, drinking and whoring, he could have left her
something. She deserved it. I was given the opportunity to go to his funeral,
but I declined. I wanted to remember him in happier times with Grandma.

Freedom

The years passed, and by the time I left the home, Father and Mother had gone their separate ways. The rest of my siblings had been sent to other children's homes and were old enough to look out for themselves.

On my sixteenth birthday, I left the home with a few possessions. I had a change of clothes, a pair of boots and shoes, and some rosary beads that one of the girls had given me as a going-away present, which I've still got.

I felt completely alone in the world.

As I walked over a bridge towards the bus stop, I spotted a duck on the water, and following her were seven baby ducklings. It brought tears to my eyes, thinking about my brothers and sisters and wondering if I would ever see them again, as I was not allowed any information as to their whereabouts. The reason given: none.

"Whoa! Hold up there! What's the rush? Where are you heading for?" It was polecat Jacqueline.

"I am supposed to get the bus to Chatham Social Services. The Mother Superior gave me three quid for the fare and for food. I'm meeting my new foster parents there. How come the nuns let you out? Weren't you supposed to become their gardener?" I said to Jacqueline Brown.

"I slaved for them for five long years. I've been punished enough for the crime I did," came her reply.

All that time in the home and I'd never asked her why she was there. She told me she had stolen money from her mother to get away from her stepfather, who was sexually abusing her. Jesus, not her as well.

"Where are you going? Back to London?" I asked her.

"I don't know; I got no family now."

I know she stank, but I felt very sorry for her. We had both been through hell in our short lives, and by now had become quite good friends.

Maybe the future would be better for us, or maybe not, I thought.

"You can come with me," I told her.

"Don't think your new foster parents would approve of that."

The bus pulled up.

"Two tickets to Chatham rail station, please."

"Rail station? Where are you going, Bridie?" asked Jacqueline.

"Home."

"And where would that be?"

"Manchester," I replied.

"Let's go!" Jacqueline squealed excitedly.

I remember the rainy streets, the place I felt so safe in, and the spirit of the people who lived there. Some would say it was a rough place, but to me it was beautiful, and I couldn't wait to get there. I had no family there anymore, but it didn't matter. After all, hadn't I survived torture and rape from a very young age? So as far as I was concerned, I came to this country and knew from day one that my young life was going to be tough, but didn't know it was going to be that tough.

But I promised myself I wouldn't let the unfortunate background stop me reaching for the stars or achieving my goals. The horrible crimes committed against me were not my fault or any other child's. I choose not to let my abuser destroy me or have any power or control over me. *He* was a bad person. My memories may still be with me, but I don't let them affect my peace of mind.

My friend Jacqueline Brown used to say I was a closed book. Now it's open for all to see. This is me, warts and all.